Quiet Girls Can Run the World

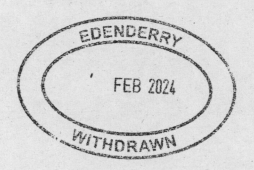

Rebecca Holman

Quiet Girls Can Run the World

The beta woman's handbook to the modern workplace

CORONET

First published in Great Britain in 2017 by Coronet
An Imprint of Hodder & Stoughton
An Hachette UK company

This paperback edition published in 2018

1

A CIP catalogue record for this title is available from the British Library

B format ISBN 9781473656215
eBook ISBN 9781473656208

Typeset in Sabon MT by Palimpsest Book Production Ltd, Falkirk, Stirlingshire

Printed and bound in Great Britain by Clays Ltd, Elcograf S.p.A.

H   l,
rene   n in
sustaina   xpected
to cor   rigin.

CONTENTS

You know that woman who isn't speaking in the meeting you're at? She's the only person who hasn't shared her thoughts on the presentation you've just watched (and you're kind of glad: you've been in the room for ninety minutes now and definitely have better things to do with your day). But her silence is in contrast to the rest of the room, and you can't work out if it's because she's intimidated (there's a lot of big personalities here), bored, disinterested, or she just doesn't have anything to say because she isn't that bright.

What you can't see is that while everyone else in the room is 'engaging in a robust exchange of views', she's making notes and thinking things through. While they're getting sucked into a pointless argument, she's trying to solve the problem. And, to save time, she'll probably email her thoughts after the meeting to the person who presented. She realises she may not get credit for solving the problem like that, but it's the easiest way to do it.

She's the Beta woman and she's getting stuff done all over your office and you probably hadn't noticed. In a world that champions shouting loudest, both IRL and online, we're told that female success in the workplace is allowed to look only a certain way: big, brash and Alpha. The reality is that any individual woman is far more complex than that, so why be so reductive?

Let's rewind. It's seven years ago. I'm in the pub on a Friday night with my new team. Two weeks before, I became their boss when I landed a job editing a women's website that had been wildly successful and was now in sharp decline. It would have taken a Herculean effort to turn it around, and as I was a relatively inexperienced, very timid editor, no one was sure if I was up to the job. Least of all me.

Apparently this was the first thing we'd all agreed on. 'They think you won't last, that you'll be out in six months,' one of my new team conspiratorially told me, in an ill-judged, booze-fuelled attempt at bonding. I stared at him aghast, my mouth hanging open. 'But I think they're wrong. There's a lot more going on there,' he added quickly, when he realised his attempt to be named Employee of the Month had backfired. 'Still waters run deep, and all that.' As he rambled on, my face felt hot and I flushed. What if they were right? If they all thought that, surely they *must* be right.

If it hadn't been Friday night I would have resigned immediately. Instead I got annihilated and did some pretty horrific snot-crying on the night bus home, accompanied by a dark cloud of self-doubt that lasted far beyond my hangover.

Two years later, it's about 11 a.m. on a Tuesday morning in November. I'm in the back of a taxi and I'm struggling to breathe. Twenty minutes earlier I was in the office, having just taken some new medication for the migraines that had been plaguing me for months. Almost instantly my chest and the back of my throat had tightened in an allergic reaction.

I'm attempting to call my doctor while trying to work out whether to get the driver to take me home or to the hospital. But my overriding thought is, I've got to get back to my desk or to my laptop before anyone notices I've gone. Any anxiety I feel over the allergic reaction, or any concern at having had three migraines every week for the last eight, is overridden by the fear that I'll be found out for what I am: not passionate enough, not committed enough, not anything enough for my job. That I don't deserve it.

A migraine isn't a good enough reason not to reply immediately to an email, and a trip to A and E no excuse for missing a deadline. Therefore I'm failing.

Last year I worked something out. I realised that, although I have very few of the obvious qualities one imagines an editor will possess – at least in the Meryl Streep, *Devil Wears Prada* vein (sharp suit, icy stare) – I'm okay at my job. Scratch that: I'm good at my job. But I only got okay, then good at it, when I worked out that embracing who I was and what I was good at, rather than pretending to be someone else, was the only thing that was going to work. The minute I stopped questioning whether I was the right person for the role and focused on doing the job, everything fell into place. Basically, I embraced my inner Beta.

But you don't have to do it my way – spending the best part of a decade sweaty-palmed in meetings, panicking every Sunday night and penning imaginary resignation letters twice weekly . . .

As it happens, I'd never seen myself as an editor. I'd always known I wanted to write, and as I studied journalism and applied diligently for work experience, I pictured myself as a staff writer somewhere – researching stories, doing interviews, and filing my copy to a shadowy editor figure, who didn't really feature in my fantasies of what adult life would look like. Because, as we're told, there's only one type of person who becomes the boss, and I certainly wasn't it.

After I graduated, I started working for a publishing agency in south London. We had a small team, and worked across lots of different projects. I was a decent writer, worked hard and was happy to muck in, so eventually I was made editor of my own little title (I was also the deputy editor, staff writer and editorial assistant). Then I worked on a bigger magazine, and eventually I was made editor again, with my own small team to manage.

And then the recession hit. We lost the contract for our magazine, I lost my job and, aged twenty-six, I had to work out how to be a writer, editor, and maybe even a boss outside the confines of the safe little space I'd worked in for the last four years.

With each new freelance gig, or job, I took on, I was convinced that this would be the one where I'd find my feet, where I'd feel from the outset that I was being taken seriously. But, of course, the world doesn't work like that. How highly you rate your own ability has nothing to do with the job you're in, and everything to do with your own sense of self. What I didn't realise was that, although I'd start each job disappointed that I hadn't morphed into the professional *Wunderkind* I wanted to be, I was gradually learning what success meant to me.

But I didn't understand that at the time. Instead I spent

4

the rest of my twenties and my early thirties feeling like a bad editor and a bad boss. So, what changed? In part, I got a bit older and stopped worrying. No one was trying to have me fired so I couldn't have been doing that bad a job, right? (Classic Beta self-deprecation, right there . . .)

And I got more experienced – I learnt more stuff. On the day I joined the place I work now, someone asked me a technical question to which I knew the answer. More than that, I was the only person around who did know the answer. Somehow, I'd gone from always feeling like the youngest and least experienced member of the team to the most experienced. Or, to put it another way, it took me until I was thirty-one to grasp that there were occasions when I was the most experienced person in the room.

But experience isn't really about knowing the answers. It's about being okay with not knowing the answers. And the real breakthrough for me came when I stopped reacting to what I thought other people were thinking (which is a ridiculous and pointless guessing game) and started focusing on what I wanted to achieve. Easier said than done, but if you nail that, it's truly liberating.

A huge part of this was about my embracing the Beta. Feeling okay about admitting when I didn't know something (which is easier when you realise that no one else has a clue either), or when I was making a decision based on gut instinct (because gut instinct is part of the reason they hired me) and embracing the fact that I'd probably get it wrong sometimes (there's nothing more Beta than being able to own your mistakes with good grace).

But that's all useful stuff for life in general, so why are we focusing on the workplace here?

It's only in the last sixty years or so that women have entered the workplace in any sort of meaningful way. My mother was probably one of the first generation of women who went to work as a matter of course. For her, Alpha or Beta didn't come into it. She worked in a male-dominated environment and rarely with other women. Finding her place at the office had its own challenges, but the idea that she could be more than one 'type' of woman never occurred to her. The fact that she was there, and thriving, was enough.

Almost forty years after she first joined the workplace, we're still struggling to find more than two blueprints for how a woman should be. For example, we're endlessly told that our job needs to be the centre of our universe; it has to be our passion. Clocking off at 5 p.m. isn't an option (unless you're clocking off at five to pursue your secret-passion project, which one day you intend to make your full-time career). Success at work only looks one way. And a successful woman? She's shouting louder than everyone else in the room. She's bloody-minded and argumentative because these are all signs that she's passionate about the project at hand and cares about its success above all else. *Ergo*, she's good at her job.

And where does that leave the rest of us? Those of us who ask questions before making decisions, for whom compromise isn't a dirty word but a way to make things work and drive things forward? Is wanting evenings and weekends to be about something more than a screen and work a sign of laziness? Are we by default bad at our jobs? Do we not care enough? Because that's kind of how the narrative goes right now.

But there's a good reason why women's roles in the workplace lack so much nuance – and it's why this book is about Beta women and work, not about Beta people. Men don't need to figure out where they fit in the workplace to the same extent: the workplace was created to fit around them. Men have had centuries to fine-tune how their individual personality types can survive and thrive in an office environment. Women have had just sixty years to get it right, and when we're still fighting to be paid the same amount as our male counterparts, it's no wonder that when we do smash through the glass ceiling, or even attempt to get near it, our roles become one-dimensional.

Who's got time to blaze a trail on their own terms when we've got all of this to contend with? It's exhausting.

So that's where we are: 47 per cent of the workforce reduced to being the secretary or the shoulder-pad-wearing bitch-boss. But that's not my reality and I'm guessing it's not yours either.

How do you know if you're an Alpha or a Beta woman? It's tricky, because almost every careers coach, psychologist or, indeed, woman I spoke to had a different answer when I asked them if they could explain what Alpha and Beta were, and which camp they fell into. And the fact is, we're all on a spectrum of Alpha and Betaness, but we need to start somewhere.

When I'm talking about Alpha and Beta women, this is always what I think of: you have two women in your office, both great at their jobs, but with very different personalities. One is Alpha Woman, and she possesses many of the traits we readily associate with success. She is impeccably dressed, perfectly groomed and highly organised. She is always on time and is always prepared for every meeting or presentation. She is decisive and will be the first to share her opinion in a meeting (the rest of the room will often defer to that opinion, such is her authority). She has no apparent fear of confrontation. She is highly competitive, whether she's running a marathon or working her way through the Booker Prize shortlist before anyone else. She has boundless levels of energy and enthusiasm, her social-media output is perfectly curated – in fact, she is excellent at promoting her own work and achievements via every available medium. She's focused, single-minded and will push things through even when other people don't agree with her (which means she can also be dogmatic, and will kick up a fuss when she doesn't get her own way). She's the woman in the office whom men will describe as 'scary' or 'a bitch' when they don't get their own way with her. She may be inspiring, she may be intimidating, but she's certainly Alpha. She starts the conversation, she sets the agenda. Others follow.

Got it? Right.

What about Beta? She may appear (but not always) to be less organised than her Alpha peer, but this is mainly because if she is less than prepared for a meeting, she'll certainly 'fess up to it rather than styling it out, as Alpha would. (Alpha Woman would never show weakness; Beta Woman is constantly revealing hers.) Beta Woman is an excellent team player and collaborator, and her team love her, but she's also extremely self-deprecating. When she speaks up in a meeting (the idea that a Beta Woman will sit in silence and never share her opinion is a myth: she just considers what she says beforehand), she'll qualify everything as 'opinion' rather than 'fact'. She's laid-back and feels she hasn't enough energy to be 'on' all the time, unlike her Alpha colleague. She's a hard worker – diligent – but when she's finished work for the day, she's finished. When she makes decisions they are considered and thought-out, and she tries to be as accommodating and flexible as she can, to ensure that the needs – and agendas – of as many people as possible are met. Men in the office who don't get what she's about might describe her as a 'pushover' or a 'lightweight'.

None of us will be all of either Alpha or Beta: for example, I've written what is basically the Beta description about myself, but I know I share some traits with Alpha. And plenty of classic Alpha women will, I'm sure, identify with some aspects of a Beta personality. But which of these women looks like success? Is it the quieter, considered Beta, or the decisive, make-things-happen Alpha?

It's the Alpha every time, but that's wrong. Not because the Alpha isn't doing a great job, but because we should all be able to succeed on our own terms – however loudly we shout.

I'm only just working this out, which is part of the point of this book: it's my way of finding out if I can be truly successful on my own terms, without emulating other people's model for success. But also, and more importantly, I want to champion the aforementioned Beta girl, because she's doing a great job, and no one tells her so often enough. I want to sing her praises from the rooftops, and remind us all that success can look however you want it to.

And we're going to need Beta Woman more than ever because the world is changing, fast. We need people who can lead with emotional intelligence, be flexible to new ideas and adapt their plans when required, leaving their ego at the door. Beta Woman's time is now.

So, here's to the collaborators, the pragmatists and the people who believe that being nice works, and that getting your own way isn't always the most important thing. Here's to the unsung workforce of Beta women who are being great bosses, great leaders, and are still sometimes at the front of the charge to the pub at 5.01 p.m. Because I'm sure being a superwoman is great, but it doesn't always look like the most fun.

1.

BETA WOMAN WHO?

'So who is the Beta woman? How is she different from the Alpha woman? Why are you so determined to force all working women into two unhelpful and reductive boxes?' I hear you ask.

Let's start with the latter, because it's the simplest to answer. I want to talk about Beta women not because I think all women either are or aren't one – as I've already said, it's a spectrum, with some women displaying more Alpha or Beta tendencies than others – but because I want to speak up for every woman who isn't professing to be the shout-the-loudest, dogmatic, in-the-gym-at-the-crack-of-dawn, working-all-the-hours-she-can-possibly-manage-on-very-little-sleep boss-lady. Even if she isn't your boss yet, she soon will be because she's the Alpha female, and that is how it works. And in an age of Instagram #goals and constant one-upmanship, Alpha has become shorthand for hardcore. Six-kids-and-CEO-of-a-medium-sized-multinational hardcore. Silencing-an-entire-room-of-subordinates-with-one-glance hardcore. The early-morning-spinning-class-badge-of-honour hardcore.

I should probably have gone to interview a bunch of women at a terrifying dawn gym class for this book but, suffice to say, I only ever get up before dawn if it's to catch a cheap flight somewhere hot.

Let's be clear. Some (plenty?) of women operate in that way and are perfectly happy. The problem is that operating on full pelt has become the goal we should all be aspiring to, and that's where I take issue. Why else would there be reams of articles on the internet dedicated to the morning routines, exercise regimes, travel beauty tips and wardrobe hacks of preternaturally successful women? Yes, there are plenty of meme-friendly mantras about being yourself and finding what makes you happy, but we don't live in a world where 'being content' is a marker of success. A marker of success is zipping across town in an Uber to three different networking events before heading home to finish work and grab a refreshing four hours' sleep before it all begins again. It's exhausting and unsustainable for most mere mortals, yet anything less, and we haven't quite nailed life.

So by Beta, I mean the rest of us – the non-Alphas.

We all know who the apparent Alpha women in our lives and newsfeeds are, but who are the non-Alphas? We're the women for whom no promotion is worth getting out of bed before seven-thirty on a Monday morning. We're the women who may or may not love our jobs (although I have to confess to adoring mine) but want the opportunity to succeed and do well, so we work hard. It's women like me, who fear that they're not hardcore enough but that the time and energy they'd waste on pretending to be hardcore could be better used elsewhere . . . like on their actual job.

Just found out you've got to run a team and you're concerned that the only management style that works is the Shouting and Fear Method™? Been told you're too passive in that shouty weekly meeting where nothing ever gets decided? Can't be bothered to hang around in the office till 8 p.m. because that's what everyone else does, or Instagram your Sunday-afternoon 'mini brainstorm for next week!' session (because you're in the pub on a Sunday afternoon, where you belong, and you got all of your work finished on Friday anyway)? Then, my friend, you might just be a non-Alpha. Welcome to the club.

In this 24/7, Instagram-filtered, heavily curated world, we're told to go hard or go home – but why do we assume that going hardcore is always the best way? What are the differences between Alpha and Beta traits, and does it stand that Alpha characteristics make one more successful?

When I asked all the women I interviewed for this book if they were an Alpha or a Beta, almost no one had a straight answer for me. No one said they were an outright Alpha. Most felt they were Alpha in some aspects of their lives and Beta in others. And, equally, someone with emotional intelligence can be an excellent leader whether they're an Alpha or a Beta, but they certainly generate very different management and working styles.

At the extreme end of the spectrum, the portrayal of the Alpha woman we're used to in popular culture is not positive: it's the classic bitch or manipulator, from Cruella de Vil to Sigourney Weaver's Katharine Parker in *Working Girl*.

The reality is obviously more nuanced. Eddie Erlandson, co-author of *Alpha Male Syndrome*, characterises the Alpha woman as 'the velvet hammer . . . they maybe have a little higher EQ (Emotional Quotient, or Emotional Intelligence) [than Alpha males] . . . but they can be equally as urgent, assertive and aggressive as men are'. So, the

Alpha female could be less obviously identifiable than her male counterpart, because she will be more inclined to wind in her Alpha-ness when the situation requires, but still possesses the same drive and assertiveness.

And, of course, there are many examples of the classic Alpha woman in popular culture and current affairs – it makes sense that Alpha women will, by definition, be the ones we all know about. Think Beyoncé, Hillary Clinton and Madonna.

So what's the difference between an Alpha and a Beta woman? A Beta woman is 'more likely to be the one who isn't taking accolades,' explains Nicole Williams, careers expert at Works. 'Instead she's saying, "Look at what my colleagues did . . ." The Beta is more receptive. They aren't dogmatic.' Or as *The Urban Dictionary* puts it: 'The Beta female will be called upon to voice her opinions, and her evaluations will most times be valued by the Alpha female. She also knows when to keep silent and when to talk. She is second in command.'

It's harder to find IRL examples of Beta women in popular culture – Beta women's tendency to work for the group rather than personal glory will put paid to that. (Jennifer Aniston's name is often bandied around as the celebrity example of choice, pitted against Angelina Jolie's Alpha, but I'm not buying it.) Then there are the *faux*-Betas, whose #relatable 'real' persona no doubt hides an Alpha-worthy hide of steel (Taylor Swift, I'm looking at you). But more on *faux*-Betas later.

Even when it comes to fictional female characters, the Beta is rarely at the forefront. One exception that springs to mind is Helen Fielding's Bridget Jones. The nineties poster girl for 'normal women' is about as Beta as they come, but maybe that's because her life is presented to us in diary format – we get to read every thought she has. Every insecurity, moment of self-doubt, loneliness or fear is laid out in full for us. Maybe we're all a Beta in the pages of our diaries.

We're told – in a nutshell – that being Beta is all about being a professional sidekick. The perpetual Robin to an Alpha's Batman. Betas are often perceived as weak, embodying the female traits we don't consider to be powerful or valuable in the workplace: empathy, collaboration, the ability to listen. But does being a woman mean that you're statistically more likely to be Beta? Sort of. Ish.

Research by Erlandson and his wife and co-author, Kate Ludeman, found that men are more socially conditioned to embody Alpha traits than women, and Alpha women are likely to possess fewer 'Alpha risk factors' than men. HR consultant Tanya Hummel agrees: 'We're talking about Alpha versus Beta but it could just as well be men versus women, because as much as you do get the Queen Bee who pulls the rungs up behind her, you also find that [women leaders] tend to be good coaches and that everyone wants to work with them because they're collaborative, they're accommodating. They allow creativity because they're less aggressively competitive than if you were in an all-male environment.'

Hummel also explained that about two-thirds of those identified in personality tests as being people-focused and -oriented (a classic Beta trait I have in spades) will be women. Meanwhile, two-thirds of those who are much more outcome-focused (a more classic Alpha trait) tend to be men. Not all men or women fall into either category, but there is a gender bias.

And although Alpha women like to win, most experts agree that they tend (on the whole) to be less belligerent and authoritarian than their male counterparts. And if you believe that Alpha or Beta is about learned behaviour as much as about genetics, then few would argue against the premise that women are still taught to embody more classically Beta behaviour than men.

Dr Marianne Cooper, sociologist at the Clayman Institute for Gender Research and lead researcher for *Lean In* by Sheryl Sandberg, prefers to think about personality types in terms of agentic versus communal ('agentic' being direct, ambitious, self-starter, forceful, and 'communal' as, her words, 'nice and warm and friendly'). 'With these two different sets of behaviours, the agentic are strongly associated with men, and what culturally we think men are like, and the communal are the same but in women, so this is the root of stereotypes about men and women. And as there's so much belief and understanding that you really have to be type A in order to be a leader, that's where we arrive at this place where leadership is seen as a better match for men.

'So the problem for women is, if they engage in these sort of alpha or agentic behaviours, they're violating expectations about how women are supposed to behave and they get pushed back for it. And then women who exhibit the marking in all characteristics – the ones we expect and associate with women – they're often not taken seriously and they're seen to be less competent.'

It's a double bind.

And here's why this book is about Beta women and not Beta men. Those same traits that women are taught and conditioned to embody, from being accommodating and flexible, to being nurturing and pragmatic, are often the same traits that are dismissed in the workplace as a sign that one is not 'serious' or 'competitive' enough or 'doesn't have the edge'.

'There's a very narrow framework through which we allow people to be leaders and display their sense of leadership, and I think it narrows even more for women and people of colour,' says Dr Cooper.

The traits that are found more often in women than in men (and before a squillion Alpha women write to me in outrage, I appreciate that this won't apply to everyone) aren't those that are considered traditional makers of success.

There's a simple reason why our view of success is so bizarrely narrow. Men have always dominated the workplace – and still do. Of course we automatically – wrongly – use traditionally male traits as markers for professional success and rarely question it. That's how it's always been.

But it's plain wrong. The markers of success, of a good boss, of a productive employee or a successful entrepreneur, are far more complex than how Alpha you are. Otherwise this would be a very short book indeed.

For starters, according to Nicole Williams, being a Beta can make you a better leader than an Alpha. 'As a manager, it's your role to make other people shine,' she explains. 'And one of the great boss-like characteristics of Betas is that they bring out the best in others.'

I asked dozens of women of different ages, working in

different industries, to tell me about the characteristics they most admired in their past bosses and managers and to describe some of their key traits. Their responses were strikingly similar. Almost everyone talked of people who gave them clear objectives and tracked their progress, but didn't micromanage them. And almost everyone mentioned a boss who was smart and inspiring. The more important traits were almost always empathy and the ability to be inspired by their team; the great boss didn't harbour unrealistic expectations or make hardcore demands.

People remember the bosses who gave them the direction and freedom to do the best job they could and encouraged their personal development. You know, the team players, the nurturers. The Betas.

At the moment we're seeing, more than ever, how dynamic Alpha leadership doesn't always translate into a good management style. In early 2017, Uber's CEO Travis Kalanick was forced to apologise after he was caught on camera having a heated exchange with a driver during a night out. The driver complains about the company's pay rates and business model, to which Kalanick can be heard saying, 'Some people don't like to take responsibility for their own shit. They blame everything in their life on somebody else. Good luck!'

The company has since been plagued with numerous claims of sexual harassment and dodgy HR practices, so this incident is potentially a drop in an ocean of toxic behaviour. Kalanick comes across as the worst type of Silicon Valley bro, but when the video came out he was contrite: 'By now I'm sure you've seen the video where I treated an Uber driver disrespectfully. To say that I am ashamed is an extreme understatement. My job as your leader is to lead, and that starts with behaving in a way that makes us all proud. That is not what I did, and it cannot be explained away.'

Kalanick went on to say that he'd realised he needed to change as a leader and receive help. We have no way of knowing how sincere he was in his apology, but it's interesting that he knew he needed to make it, that his brash, arrogant (and extreme Alpha) leadership model wasn't impressing anyone even if it worked for him (and his investors) in Uber's fast-moving, fast-growing early years.

Similarly, Miki Agrawal, the dynamic female founder of Thinx, an online female-hygiene company, faced accusations of sexual harassment from staff in early 2017. Aside from the allegations, it was noted that as the company quickly grew Agrawal failed to employ any HR staff or implement HR policy. She later stood down as CEO, to focus on promoting the brand, saying, 'I'm *not* the best suited for the operational CEO duties, nor was it my passion to be so.'

Tinder, Airbnb, Snapchat – the small, agile tech start-ups of yore, where big ideas, even bigger vision and brash arrogance ruled the day – are now fully fledged businesses, with HR practices, shareholders and customer expectations to adhere to. And what we're seeing is that some of the big Alpha bosses who got the businesses off the ground aren't necessarily the right people to see them through the next ten, twenty, thirty years.

It's not just about the tech industry either. I heard a story about a creative, dynamic, energetic and Alpha CEO, who had the vision, drive and energy to transform a large publishing house's fortunes when they needed a total change of direction. Later, when the company was in 'business as usual' mode, she was let go, and replaced with a much more process-driven, quieter Beta leader. The reason? She was amazing when huge, disruptive changes had to happen, but couldn't manage people properly or keep things ticking over on a day-to-day basis.

You want someone to steady the ship? Get a Beta in.

But Betas are timid, shy and introverted, right? How can they ever be leaders? After the publication of Susan Cain's brilliant *Quiet: The Power of Introverts in a World That Can't Stop Talking*, much was made of how overlooked the introvert has become in the workplace. But it's wrong to say that an extrovert is always an Alpha and a Beta the opposite, although there are some big areas of crossover. Nicole Williams agrees: 'What makes people extroverted doesn't always make them a leader and vice versa, and charisma and magnetism can be taught and learned,' she explains.

But there is a difference. While your Alpha or Beta-ness is to do with your position within a group, your work team or a friendship circle, your response to being around other people depends on your extroversion or introversion. Simply put, extroverts gain energy from being around other people, and introverts find it drains them.

Many of the characteristics found in introverts may also be found in Beta women, but equally they may not. As it happens, I'm an introvert, but a fairly outgoing one. I find it intensely draining to spend all my time around other people, and although being in a room full of people I don't know isn't my favourite thing, I can handle it. To some

Alphas, though, a party where they know just one person is a source of extreme anxiety.

And, as I can't emphasise enough, when it comes to personality types, few of us sit on either extreme end of the scale and most of the women I know who are characteristically Alpha have the emotional intelligence to switch between the two as necessary: they can read a room. But none of this explains why we persist with the myth that Alpha is better.

It's important because if – like me – you don't fall into that tiny subset of people who are Alpha all the time, you'll never feel you're doing enough or good enough. We all have the persistent inner voice that tells us we're not good enough – and when you're constantly being told that your personality fundamentally doesn't fit the job you're doing, that voice can be impossible to ignore. Your self-worth at work becomes about who you are, not about what you're doing.

I hate conflict, but for years my inner voice would tell me that I wasn't passionate enough because I didn't get into screaming rows with my editorial team over every feature. Striving for consensus meant I was putting people-pleasing above doing my job, and being nice meant I was a pushover. For ages I couldn't get past the idea that to be a good leader – someone people look up to and trust – you have to be at the front, shouting the loudest, and possibly throwing a desk lamp out of the window when things don't go your way.

This has always been rubbish, but never more so than now. Times are changing: we live in a world where the hard skills we learnt just ten or even five years ago at university or in training are fast becoming obsolete. In a world where the pace of technology makes the concept of a job for life laughable. Right now, I'm thirty-four, and Facebook didn't exist when I was at university. Social media (or, indeed, digital content) didn't feature when I did my journalism training. Now if a lecturer in journalism didn't encourage their students to understand and be fully prepared for a digital world, it would be neglectful, never mind remiss.

Similarly, setting up your own business without a website, or without understanding social media as a vital tool in reaching your customers, is now unthinkable. Fifteen years ago, an online presence was an after-thought. Fifteen years is no time at all, when you consider that we'll all be working until we're seventy.

So, yes, being 'really good at shouting' is great, but to survive the twenty-first-century workplace you need to be flexible and you need to be able to face change head on. Which is why the so-called 'soft skills' found in women (specifically Beta women) – emotional intelligence, the ability to work with people, pragmatism – are becoming increasingly prized.

In fact, the World Economic Forum's 2016 job report highlighted emotional intelligence as one of the top ten skills required in the workplace by 2020, alongside persuasion and teaching others – all strong Beta skills.

With all of this in mind, why do we insist upon such a narrow portrayal of success and successful women in popular culture, in the media and even in how we present ourselves to others via social media? It's because we still accept as fact several untruths about workplace culture, which cloud everything that comes after.

When I was a child, my mother (who was very good at her job) used to work long hours – often leaving before we woke up in the morning and not returning until long after we'd gone to bed. She was company secretary to an engineering firm. She was lucky in that she was well rewarded for her hard work with a career that paid well and offered clear progression – plenty of people work just as hard without anything like the benefits.

But despite spending most of her career in environments where gruelling long hours were the norm, her takeaway to me when I first started working was 'There's no glory in working late.' She certainly wasn't saying sack off work at five on the dot, irrespective of what else is going on. What she meant was, no one notices or cares if you're working late (or, to put it another way, a good boss shouldn't be mentally totting up team Brownie points based on how late it is when you get all your work done: they should be querying why you have so much to do that you can't get it done in a working day). And we automatically assume that if other people are staying late, it must be because they're incredibly busy or working so much harder than we are. But maybe they're staying behind to work on another project, or spent half their day watching reality TV and need to stay late to catch up on their work.

But the basic message is simple: attribute working long to working hard at your peril.

There are numerous studies into the link between productivity and hours worked, and the correlation is clear: the fewer hours someone works, the more productive they are in that time. In an experiment conducted by Gothenburg City Council over two years, nurses at the Svartedalen retirement home in the city switched from an eight-hour to a six-hour working day for the same wage to see if a six-hour working day would boost productivity. It concluded that fewer hours' work led to more productive staff (and that the staff working six hours a day were far less likely to take sick days than those working the standard eight – although the scheme was later scrapped when the council concluded that the associated costs of hiring seventeen extra staff for the duration of the experiment outweighed the benefits). Meanwhile a survey in the UK revealed that six out of ten British bosses believed that cutting the working day from eight to six hours would be beneficial for productivity.

But if you've just come back to work feeling refreshed after a long weekend, taken a sneaky afternoon off work because you can't bear to look at your screen any more, or noticed how much of a zombie you now are on a Friday afternoon, you knew that already, didn't you?

Rob Yeung, an organisational psychologist at consultancy Talentspace, agrees: 'Particularly for people who think it's very important to go home and spend time with their family and friends, or do things other than their nine-to-five jobs, then, yes, the longer you need to stay the more you may resent it and you may feel less productive. You can feel anxious, and even experience burnout.'

All excellent reasons why sticking around at work until stupid o'clock is rubbish for productivity, and why, as a boss, terrorising your team into staying late is a Bad Idea.

Yeung adds, 'In an ideal world, yes, your boss should care if they have an employee who's regularly having to stay late at work – and there's good research showing that bosses who have greater empathy and provide greater support tend to get more productivity and hard work out of their employees. But there are many organisations in which staying late seems stitched into the fabric of the culture. I know that many people, particularly in professional service industries such as finance, law, and management consultancy, feel compelled to stay late because everyone else seems to be doing it. In those cases, trying to get away early has to be a careful balancing act.

'Yes, by all means leave early if you are certain that your performance is above average. But if you have been told that your performance is somewhat lacking, or you're at all unsure how you're perceived in the workplace, it may not be a good idea to leave earlier than your colleagues.'

Numerous productivity studies over the years have shown that it's the people with less time to spend in the office (such as mothers working part time or rushing to leave at five on the dot so they can do the nursery pick-up) who use it most productively. (And a 2010 study in the *European Heart Journal* found that if you spend more than ten hours a day in the office, you're 60 per cent more likely to have a heart attack. Argh.) Being able to delegate, to make thoughtful decisions quickly, to prioritise work for yourself and your team are all signs that you're a banging boss. And yet . . . and yet . . . Starting work at 7 a.m. is still seen as a badge of honour, especially if you've managed to get in an Instagram of that networking event you made it to the night before. Because . . . hardcore.

And the really stupid thing is, all those productivity studies are looking at whether we should be working fewer than the standard eight hours, while actually we're working far more than that already. From the extra hour or so you habitually clock up in the office, to the constant checking of emails in the evening, or logging on to finish a few things off, we're always on, and we're always expected to be on, and it's frying out brains.

I made Alyss, who works for me, switch off the emails on her phone when she was on holiday because she kept replying to things and checking them. 'It's not that there was anything in particular I'd left undone, or that I needed to do. It's just that other people were emailing me in the expectation that I'd reply, so I felt like I had to.'

It's not necessarily that we all have so much work to do that we can't get it done in any given forty-hour week. It's that when everyone else is plugged in, constantly emailing and constantly on, your opting out marks you as less than committed – especially when your boss or direct line manager is always on and expects the same from you.

Getting tired, needing a day away from our desks and demonstrating anything less than slavish enthusiasm for our jobs are all frowned upon. Not because that's real life, but because we have such a narrow spectrum for what success looks like.

MYTH 2. SHE (OR HE) WHO SHOUTS LOUDEST PROBABLY KNOWS WHAT THEY'RE TALKING ABOUT

Ever noticed that if no one in the room really knows what they're talking about, they instantly defer to the one person who's talking loudly and authoritatively about the matter at hand? Whether there's any value in what they're saying is irrelevant. It's far better to have an instant, definitive opinion on everything than to say nothing at all. The result? People with loud voices, who tend not to think before they speak, often assume positions of power or authority.

It's often why people clamour to criticise an idea, pitch or project they don't really understand: it's better to get in there first and say something than to keep schtum. I've certainly done it myself. I can think of more than one occasion when an external person has pitched or presented to me and I've responded by listing all the things I didn't like about it. On one occasion, I'm ashamed to say, I made the presenter so nervous that she fluffed the meeting. I could just as easily have started with the good stuff in a constructive conversation rather than a barrage of negativity. But what if you don't have a chance to get your criticism in and people subsequently think you're too nice or a pushover? We can't have that, can we, ladies?

It's something I'm hyper-aware of, and I still find myself doing it on occasion. And the end result is that we mistake the volume of someone's voice, and the frequency with which they speak up in meetings, as competence. We also end up assuming that people who are particularly extroverted, outspoken by nature, good at public speaking, or who are just really chatty, are the ones who know what they're doing. Of course one can be all of these things *and* incredibly competent, it's just that they're not mutually inclusive traits. Being outgoing or even a loudmouth is a personality trait, not a mark of intelligence or judgement (the flipside, of course, is that being quiet or shy doesn't make you an idiot or an automatic genius: the two just aren't linked).

MYTH 3. GOOD MANAGERS NEVER GET EMOTIONAL, AND KEEP THEMSELVES AT ARM'S LENGTH FROM THEIR TEAM. THIS IS ESPECIALLY TRUE FOR WOMEN

To be authoritative as a woman, you have to be something of a cold fish, right? This is why so many famously powerful and authoritative (fictional) women are depicted as such – and why so many prominent, successful IRL women are portrayed in such a cartoonish way by the media. If you show an interest in your team's life outside work, engage with them on a personal level, or show any other evidence of caring about the people who work for or with you, you're in danger of giving in to your almost uncontrollable maternal instincts. Next thing you know, you'll be handing out pay rises to female members of staff for being really stoic during their periods and rewarding male members of your team with a special bonus if they get in before midday when they've got a really bad hangover. Because you're a woman, you're either a bleeding-heart walkover or an ice queen.

To demonstrate authority, to be a 'good' boss, to be 'good' at your job in general, you must, supposedly, be the latter. Ruling through fear is how proper (Alpha) career women do business: if you're genuinely busy and important, you won't have time for the niceties, or to consider other people's feelings. Being nice, saying 'please' and persuading rather than telling people to do what you need are signs you've got too much time on your hands. After all, getting your subordinates (or colleagues) to do something for you because they like you and you've asked nicely is a total cop-out – right?

*

Now I've obviously signposted that these myths aren't true (for starters, I've called them myths, which should be your first clue) because they're so ridiculous. But in the real world, with all its unspoken rules and social nuances, they're not. I bet if you're a woman who has been at work at some point, you'll recognise at least a grain of truth among the silliness. It's so insidious we barely notice it's happening, but among all the progress ostensibly being made in the workplace, it's still there. The way women are viewed (and the way we view other women) at work is still binary. You're Alpha or Beta. You're good at your job or bad at it, and never the twain shall meet.

You see, you have to be one of those two broad personality types, just like you have to be either the loudmouth or the mouse, the hardcore workaholic or the flake – because how else will people make snap judgements about whether you're good at your job or not, based on no firm evidence?

But the thing is, Alpha and Beta behaviour, in its modern form, is learnt behaviour: it's not hardwired into our DNA (apart from anything else, all typical Alpha traits that would have been useful to caveman Alpha, like 'being really good at hunting bison', have limited practical application in, say, a career in the City).

In fact, Eddie Erlandson believes that our Alpha and Beta traits are all part of different personas that people develop in childhood. Women are more likely to develop Beta traits than men, in behaviour learnt from childhood, and are capable of switching it on or off. 'I think you can see Alpha traits by age three,' he explains. 'Now you could say, if you see them that clearly, they must somehow be communicated through the genetic pathways. On the other hand, remember that people are learning all their key styles around security, approval and safety before the age of six, so they are picking up a tremendous amount from the environment around them, whether that be parents or uncles or siblings or whatever.'

Erlandson found that explaining this to Alpha clients actually had a liberating effect – 'It helps them see their behaviour as a collection of habits that were formed early in their lives rather than as an unchangeable genetic trait.'

I like this theory: it feels far more attuned to how we actually live our lives than the idea that women are constantly having to fake professionalism to fight their almost overpowering maternal instinct.

The fact is, we're all capable of operating on a broad spectrum of Alpha and Beta behaviour, and doing so is a far better representation of our true personalities than the one-note parody of the classic Alpha or Beta.

And, of course, most people are more complex than one of the two broad, lazy categories all women are assigned to, but that's how we're assigned nonetheless. Alpha or Beta, workaholic or work-shy, good or bad.

It means that we're supposedly failing if we're not the most accomplished woman in the room. It means that succeeding on our own terms doesn't count: we're only winning if we've beaten everyone else. Picture the classic Alpha woman. It's such a narrow definition that it can't possibly represent more than 5 per cent of the population (mostly white, professional, middle-class Western women). I keep hearing about this woman and her many achievements because versions of her probably take up a disproportionate amount of space on my social-media newsfeeds (and the rest of us are emulating this behaviour because we feel we should), but does she represent all women? Of course not.

And, in fact, when I remember the dozens of supremely talented, inspiring, successful women I've worked with over the last decade, I can think of only a couple who come close to the classic Alpha role. Now, they are great bosses and great people. But so are all the others. And yet we're told if we're not one of the 5 per cent, we're not doing enough, and we're not good enough.

So this is for the other 95 per cent of us. Because there's more than one way to absolutely boss it at work, and I'm going to prove it.

2.

Who's your Beta role model? Hillary Clinton? Oh, come on, she's the most famous Alpha on the planet. Taylor Swift? She's such an Alpha that she can lord it over her own squad – although she can switch to Beta-ness which can actually bolster her personal image. Or maybe it's Emma Watson. You know, Hermione. She's pretty Beta, right? Well, I think she demonstrates a laser-like focus that implies an Alpha personality. We just assume she's 'quiet' (Beta) because she doesn't give many interviews.

Alpha women are all we see, not that you'd always know it. There's a weird disconnect between women on television, in films or in politics and the personas they use. Because relatability – the ability to appear 'normal' and 'just like the rest of us' – has become like fairy dust for anyone with a public persona, from politicians to celebrities. Hillary Clinton was lampooned before the 2016 election for not being relatable enough. (Incidentally, would a male politician have had to go so far to prove they were 'real'? Probably not: no one worried about that picture of Donald Trump posing outside his gold lift after winning an election campaign he fought on the basis that he wasn't part of the 'elite'.

Similarly, actresses like Jennifer Lawrence, and comedians and writers like Tina Fey and Amy Schumer saw their careers skyrocket because, apart from being supremely talented, they were also seen as 'real' and 'fallible' and crucially 'normal'.

And 'normal', of course, is lazy shorthand for what we'd probably imagine a Beta woman to be. It's the quirky hot mess, the pizza-eating Oscar fall-overer (Jennifer Lawrence, I'm looking at you). Even Taylor Swift, whose micro-managed personal image, prodigious output and schedule are the very definition of Alpha, still wants us to know how cute and normal she is. Because Alpha means you're trying hard, Alpha means you want it too much, and no one's going to admit to that. Similarly, Alpha means you're not relatable: you're not like the people you're selling your wares to – you don't get them, so they won't get you.

It's like that age-old question (age-old if you're me, anyway). Why do people love Jennifer Lawrence but dislike Anne Hathaway? J-Law can do no wrong, whether she's papped enjoying what appears to be a large spliff and an even larger glass of wine on a hotel balcony, or face-planting at yet another awards do, she's the ultimate woman of the people. Yes, she's a preternaturally beautiful, Oscar-worthy actress, but she also has the same foibles as the rest of us (the same photogenic foibles anyway: we're still waiting for the leaked video of her picking her nose or squeezing her blackheads). Yet when Anne Hathaway, another incredibly beautiful, talented and indeed Oscar-worthy actress, revealed that she'd practised her Oscars acceptance speech in 2013 to make herself seem more likeable, it turned people off her: that wasn't 'real', it was 'try hard'.

Journalist Ann Friedman discussed this phenomenon in a 2013 article she wrote for the *Cut*:

When she [Jennifer Lawrence] jokes about sucking in her stomach on the red carpet or her publicist hating her for eating a Philly cheesesteak ('There's only so much Spanx can cover up!'), it feels real, not designed to fool her fans into thinking she's not one of those salad-but-hold-the-dressing girls. Lawrence said she ordered a McDonald's on the red carpet at the Oscars.

Hathaway is a vegan.

The problem, Friedman opines, is that we just don't find seemingly perfect, successful women particularly likeable:

Hathaway, who has been acting for a decade and was a clear favorite for the Best Supporting Actress award, seems to fit the broader cultural pattern (I've called it the Hillary Catch-22) in which we simply don't find successful, 'perfect' women very likable. Lawrence is well aware that it serves her well to stay the underdog.

When a celebrity stops being relatable, we fall out of love with them. When their life becomes too perfect, they start to sound too media-trained. When they become too slick, we no longer compare ourselves to them in a favourable way – they start to make us feel bad about ourselves. And then they get the Anne Hathaway treatment.

So Beta equals relatable, relatable equals popular, and the more popular you are as a woman in the limelight, the more bankable you are as a star. Pitch it right, and being a Beta is big business.

But let's be real. Jennifer Lawrence is surviving and thriving in the cut-throat world of Hollywood. Amy

Schumer and Tina Fey cut their teeth in the male-dominated writers' room at *Saturday Night Live* before joining the boys on stage. Is an actress, writer or comedian who's especially Beta capable of doing all those things? Of course. Do we live in a culture where a Beta woman would be given the time and space to thrive in those environments? I really don't think so.

Because here's the paradox. To make it as a female actress, writer, comedian or musician, you need to have the sort of tunnel-vision determination and penchant for self-publicity that you'll almost only ever see in an Alpha woman. We live in a world where celebrity is cherished above all else – and the noise from people trying to reach the top is deafening. It's not an environment where a self-effacing, polite, think-before-they-speak Beta is likely to lead the way.

There are plenty of industries full of Beta women who are totally bossing it, but are they bossing it in the limelight? Probably not. And if they do happen to find themselves in the limelight, chances are they have . . . Never. Been. So. Uncomfortable. In. Their. Life.

Of course this doesn't mean there aren't any Betas in popular culture – there are plenty. It's just that they're fictional. Despite the apparent lack of Beta women in the upper echelons of Hollywood, all female-focused films will have at least one token Beta (as opposed to all other films, which don't feature women in a meaningful way at all), whether she's the female lead's kooky sidekick friend or, more notably, the female romantic lead (who will invariably be Beta, lest she try to wear the Alpha male lead's testicles as earrings at some point – that doesn't make for great cinema, apparently). And in the unlikely event that she starts off the film Alpha, we'll watch the male lead break down her Alpha-ness until she's a quivering Beta ball of lust and love. By breaking down her defences (also known as her very reasonable reservations about dating such an aggressively arrogant narcissist) and convincing her that there's more to life than her career (convincing her to ditch her appearance in a massive human-rights case to go on a mini-break with him to the Cotswolds), he's revealed her true Beta self. And now she can be the passive Beta she'd always secretly desired to be. She can be happy.

Journalist Caitlin Moran points this out in her column for *The Times Magazine*:

The parameters of jobs for women on film are pretty consistent: they should allow her to wear whatever she wants, so she can express her personality through her wacky/hot outfits (that's half of a woman's entire personality, amirite?). They should be flexible enough for the woman to sack off her duties to take part in other more romantic scenes involving her male co-star. They should allow her to be her crazy, winsome, possibly problematic-drinking self – able to blurt out whatever's on her mind, which confirms what an untameable maverick she is.

And you can't have verbal diarrhoea when you're running a large multinational, can you?

Even in films where a woman's job might actually be a plot point, it's often just that – a plot point. Her looks and romantic vulnerabilities are of far more interest to the average casting director.

There's a great Twitter account, @femscriptintros, which tweets the intros written for female characters in film scripts. Choice samples include:

> JANE (late 20s) sits hunched over a microscope. She's attractive, but too much of a professional to care about her appearance.

> JANE stands next to it (30s), dressed in a paramedic's uniform – blonde, fit, smokin' hot.

> The next candidate is JANE. She has her hair pinned back and wears glasses. In her late 20s, she's attractive in a reserved kind of way.

And we wonder why there's confusion over how women should or shouldn't behave in the workplace.

This is also borne out in the statistics. According to the Geena Davies Institute on Gender in Media, when you look at every general-audience film released in cinemas between September 2006 and September 2009, 57.8 per cent of the male characters are depicted with an occupation, compared to 31.6 per cent of the females. And although 24.6 per cent of the females held professional roles compared to 20.9 per cent of the males, the types of roles depicted are woefully narrow. Across more than three hundred speaking characters, not one female is depicted in the medical sciences (a doctor or a vet), in the top levels of senior management (CEO, CFO), in the legal world or the political arena.

The report also notes that female characters are noticeably absent from the upper echelons of power across multiple industries. Not one woman is present at the top of the business/financial sector, the legal arena or journalism. Among the fifty-eight top executives portrayed in the corporate world (CEOs, CFOs, presidents, vice presidents, general managers), only two are female (and in case you're curious as to which two female characters they're referring to, as I was, they keep the specific films anonymous to avoid shaming specific actors – soz).

Similarly, in their 2015–16 report *Boxed In*, the Centre for the Study of Women in Television and Film at San Diego State University revealed that 'Regardless of platform, gender stereotypes on television programs abound. Female characters were younger than their male counterparts, more likely than men to be identified by their marital status, and less likely than men to be seen at work and actually working.'

The report also stated that 'Overall, male characters were almost twice as likely as females to be portrayed as leaders.' Nine per cent of males but only five per cent of females were portrayed as leaders, and 'Female characters were more likely than males to have personal life-oriented goals, such as caring for others or being in a romantic relationship. In contrast men were more likely than females to have work-oriented goals.'

So what does this tell us? First, that according to Those Guys in Charge of Cinema, Alpha women are fundamentally less lovable than Beta women, and will end up all alone (not in a good way) if they carry on down this path. Second, if you are a Beta woman, your career will be a filler that will serve only to make you more attractive to the man who will become your husband because, let's face it, ending up Not Alone is your primary goal, unlike your Alpha sisters, who are too scary for love.

It's obvious that the ways in which female Alpha and Beta personalities are conveyed to us by popular culture fall far short of reality, and when you place those female characters in a working environment, the total lack of nuance is thrown into sharp relief. Apart from the fact that marked success at work in a female lead is seen as an obstacle for the male lead to overcome, there's an edict that says any female character who is, say, a bit messy, can never remember which bag she put her keys in, dresses in loud prints and favours a biker boot over a pair of massive heels will have a 'soft' job (librarian, dog groomer – although, to be fair, both of those sound like cracking jobs to me) or a job that has no reasonable chance of adequate financial compensation or promotion because it serves as an outlet for her creative frivolities (and she's going to end up with the male lead who owns a darling little flat in Putney that's simply crying out for a woman's touch so she doesn't need a job that pays her rent). The woman wearing a suit, shouting at people and adjusting her monstrous shoulder pads? She's good at her job, for sure. But she's probably miserable and lonely – how else could one introduce a ham-fisted element of personal growth into her storyline?

But does this matter? Films aren't real life, and we all know that. They're not *really* going to change how we behave in the workplace, are they?

According to the guys at the Geena Davies Institute, it

matters a lot. In their report, which focuses on gender bias in family or children's entertainment, they explain,

> Failing to represent females on screen may affect viewers in at least two different ways. For one thing, young children grow up consuming biased media messages. With time and repeated exposure, some children may come to normalize inequality in storytelling.
>
> This normalization process may 'spill over' to other arenas, where girls/young women and boys/young men fail to question or even perceive gender bias in a variety of academic, athletic, social or even occupational contexts. For another thing, the lack of gender balance on screen, if noticed, may communicate to girls that they are of less value than boys.

The same thing happens when you only ever see women in charge, or successful women behaving in a homogeneous way.

'You can't be what you can't see,' is a catch-all phrase that explains the lack of gender-diverse roles at senior level in most industries. I think it gets used a bit too simplistically to explain a complex problem, but the nub of the point definitely stands. Once something becomes accepted in popular culture, it becomes an idea that's addressed in soaps, covered in the mainstream press and your nan is talking about it. Then it becomes far easier to translate into, say, legislation, or a new HR code of conduct in your workplace, or in breaking down those unconscious biases that impact on every job interview you have, every male-dominated meeting you attend, or every time you put in for promotion.

The way we talk about actresses, the number of diverse (in every sense) female leads that make it into mainstream films, the more often women in films and on television present more than a one-dimensional version of what we think a woman in the workplace should look like, the less likely we are to treat women who work, who are your bosses and who succeed, like women.

The Miss Representation Project was set up off the back of a film of the same name that tackles this very issue. The project identifies the issue as the fact that 'The media are selling young people the idea that girls' and women's value lies in their youth, beauty and sexuality and not in their capacity as leaders. Boys learn that their success is tied to dominance, power and aggression. We must value people as whole human beings, not gendered stereotypes.'

But what happens, in reality, when those gendered stereotypes are all we see? Dr Caroline Heldman is an associate professor of politics at Occidental College, Los Angeles, and is also research director at the Geena Davies Institute. She points out that, although it's harder to measure the negative impacts of gender stereotypes in popular culture (that is, it's harder to gauge what young women are not becoming because of what they don't see on television), the positive effects are easier to measure. In this instance, the number of young women taking up archery: 'So there's been a boom in archery, female archers since 2012,' she explains. 'And it can be traced back to *Brave* [the Disney film] and Katniss [Everdeen, Jennifer Lawrence's character] in *The Hunger Games*. So we know for sure that it had a direct and immediate effect on the lives of hundreds of thousands of young girls.'

In short, how film and TV represent women is crucial in how young women's ambitions and aspirations are formed. It matters. A lot. 'Entertainment media is the largest, the biggest influencer in how we shape our lives. Entertainment global media really gets under the radar. I think that really gets into our subconscious and produces implicit gender bias and implicit racial bias. But also it tells us who the good people are, who the bad people are, it tells us who we should respect and deify and it tells us who we should villainise.'

I never saw myself becoming an editor when, in my teens and early twenties, I was envisaging what my career would look like, I always saw myself as a cog in a machine. I pictured myself working on a magazine, doing what I was told, sticking to deadlines and producing decent copy. The idea that I'd be the one setting the deadlines didn't occur to me, because I couldn't picture someone like me in that role. I'd always grown up in an environment where I was told I could achieve whatever I wanted – and I believed that, in the broad sense. I knew I was bright enough and capable enough to do most things (or, more accurately, I knew there were a lot of morons out there who had very important jobs, and I was possibly less of an idiot than some of them). But I didn't believe I was the right 'type' of person to be an editor. The only editors I came across were of the pseudo-fictional sort (ranging from the Paul Dacres and Rebekah Brookses of this world on one side of the spectrum and Anna Wintour on the other) or the actually fictional Miranda Priestly. The mythology surrounding these terrifying figures was so great that I could never equate my own future with that sort of job.

Had I read an interview in which a passionate editor waxed lyrical about the amazing feeling when you really connect with your audience on an issue you really care about, or how fantastic it is when a new writer files their copy and it's the best thing you've read all week, I might have reconsidered. But as far as I was concerned then, the job wasn't about the job, it was about the personality, and I didn't have the right one.

Of course, a more bullish Alpha woman might have thought differently: the idea of thriving in such a macho environment might have excited her and convinced her to pursue an editorship doggedly. She's probably my boss's boss's boss now. But the problem then is that you retain the homogeneity in senior positions that I've been talking about – it becomes an endless cycle. A job's probably not for you because you've never seen anyone like you doing it . . .

Jemma used to work for me. She's someone I'd massively characterise as Alpha. (I've always assumed she must have found it intensely frustrating to work for me because her boundless energy and enthusiasm was sometimes met head on by my desire to do 'one thing at a time' and 'wait and see what happens'.) She is fantastic at her job, works incredibly hard and never runs out of steam, but when I asked her how she'd define herself, she was far from emphatic.

'I spent a lot of my twenties aspiring to be an Alpha, and it probably wasn't sitting very comfortably with me because I felt that was probably going to be the only way I'd be successful. The women I saw that I aspired to be – all the women I was surrounded by in my first jobs, and probably the women that my parents were surrounded by

– were these big-personality eighties power-shouldered kind of women, so I was like "Okay, I definitely want to be like that." But it never sat that comfortably with me because I'm really awkward in situations of conflict – I just really hate it, and then I'm very bad at competition, like I have no desire to win really.'

Then she says something that really resonates with me: 'I spent a lot of that time in my early twenties lying in bed with my heart beating fast and analysing what had happened that day and thinking, Oh, fuck it, because I thought I hadn't dealt with a situation hard enough, or pushed it, or worked hard enough. I also think I definitely defined a lot of my life around work.' I did this too – for years. And I can pretty much guarantee that Jemma was not, by any stretch of the imagination, underperforming at work while she was worrying so much about it. But what she was worrying about – and what I worried about so much – wasn't about performance or achievement: it was about not being the right 'type' of person. Because we're taught that success is a personality type, not a mark of achievement.

And it's not just about how women deal with their own aspirations. The sort of job a female lead in a major block-buster or soap holds matters because the men we work with also see these films, watch those soaps and have to adhere to the same HR codes of conduct that we do. If your male colleague, employee or boss believes that you're only demonstrating your authority when you're shouting at someone and you don't enjoy shouting at people, how will you ever exert your authority?

It matters because women's voices simply aren't being

heard on their own terms. Numerous studies have shown that women are interrupted far more in meetings than men, as well as in the classroom and the doctor's surgery – as a 2004 study from Harvard Law School and a 1998 study by the University of California Santa Cruz demonstrated respectively. And, according to a study by Princeton and Brigham Young University, if women talk 25–50 per cent of the time in a professional meeting, they are seen as 'dominating the conversation'. A 2014 study at George Washington University found that when men were talking with women, they interrupted 33 per cent more often than when they were talking with men. The men interrupted their female conversational partners 2.1 times during a three-minute conversation. That dropped to 1.8 when they spoke to other men.

Similarly, studies show that while men in leadership positions are seen in a positive light when they demonstrate traditionally Alpha leadership traits (so, being decisive, dominating the conversation, being dogged and dogmatic in the pursuit of goals), women who demonstrate traditional Alpha leadership traits are viewed negatively by both men and women. And while men who have a more relaxed or Beta style of management are still seen in a positive light, female Beta managers aren't considered at all – because Beta women can't be managers. But why are we so unwilling to compare the relative merits of different personality types in female managers?

It's simple. It's because until comparatively recently female managers were a rarity (or an oddity, depending on how you want to define it). Relatively speaking, women's mainstream presence in the workplace, particularly our existence in white-collar management positions, is in its infancy. Our fascination with what makes our male boss tick and with how to get the most out of our male employees is long-standing.

If we want to move things on and make proper progress, popular culture is key. The homogeneous nature of female personalities in film and television – especially how they're depicted in the workplace – has a huge impact on how we view women at work.

It's not just about women believing they can do those senior roles that we're always told require a sharp suit and a sharp tongue. It's about our colleagues, bosses and employees, male or female, believing we can too.

Kesstan Blandin is the director of research at the Centre for Applications of Psychology Type, which uses the Myers Briggs Type Indicator (MBTI) as a tool to further our understanding of different personality types. (You know those personality tests you sometimes have to take as part of a job interview? You might well be taking the MBTI.) She agrees that our view of what a good leader looks like is limited, which can leave women feeling boxed in. 'It's true that women [in leadership positions] may be seen more as nasty women, a bitch, that type of thing, and not seen as strong but seen as shrill. And it's both men and women who will judge women like that, so it's a double hit.'

She also explains that our view of an archetypal leader is still severely limited to the Alpha male model. 'The cultural type ideal in America is ESTJ – so an extroverted, sensing, thinking, judging type – and . . . the stereotype or the archetype, is the military general, you know, someone who gets things done, and that's very masculine, very male.'

Blandin goes on to explain that a 'lopsided majority' of leaders in American organisations will have a combination of TJ (thinking, judging) in their personality type – so that's someone who is 'objective and rational in their decision-making. TJ is typically a very decisive style and that's what we like. We like leaders who are very sure of themselves, who are very decisive and very tough and impervious to emotional pleading, because that gets in the way.'

The result is that women are typically viewed as a sidekick to an Alpha male leader – or, as Blandin puts it, 'Women are left in the position of being the type that flatters and supports the leading man.' I interviewed her before the 2016 American election, and she mused on the possibility that those hegemonic views of men and women in leadership positions might shift. If the subsequent results are any sort of bellwether for this (and whether they are or not is subject for debate) then they're not shifting particularly quickly.

But what is it really like to work where there are few other women – and none in a senior position?

Yasmin, twenty-nine, is an engineer, operating in the energy industry. She's worked in power stations, offshore at times, and is currently managing a team of six – five of whom are men, who are older than she is.

'For my entire career I've always been the only or one of the only women sitting in a meeting, or in any situation – so for my trips offshore, I was the only woman there. I make a point of counting how many people are in the room and what the percentage of women is.' One thing that Yasmin notices when she's in a male-dominated environment is the type of language that's used. 'It's very macho and it makes me laugh because I can't take it seriously when people are going "Oh, we've got to put pressure on them," and "We've got to deliver," rather than "What's our aim and how do we help each other get there?"' Yasmin's talking specifically about gender here, but to me she's perfectly described the difference between an Alpha and a Beta in the workplace.

But how much does language matter? Yes, it sounds pretty stupid to talk like you're on Wall Street when you're heading up the accounts department of a paper manufacturer in Kettering, but words are just words, aren't they?

Yasmin thinks it goes far deeper than this: 'When I look at businesses that maybe fail, I blame egos, because you'll have a manager who'll just come out with "We're going to make X amount of money in the next five years," and they'll stick to that because that's what they've said. Then they can't see the truth and back down.'

An environment that's about 'do or die' – even in terms of the language used – quickly becomes one in which mistakes aren't tolerated and lessons aren't learnt. And anyone who's worked in that sort of environment knows how dangerous it can become. 'It makes people not admit that they don't know something,' explains Yasmin. 'And it's a culture of pretending you know what's going on when you might not – and, in fact, a lot of those around you don't know what's going on either. And I don't like that.'

Introducing more women into senior roles doesn't instantly mean that you get a more Beta environment (and plenty of women I've spoken to who work on all-female, but very Alpha, teams admit that this has challenges that aren't dissimilar to the ones Yasmin faces on a male team) but having a more diverse leadership team naturally means you're balancing out dominant personality traits and creating a more balanced environment. Few people would disagree with the idea that collaboration and teamwork are key to a team's or a project's success, yet we're never going to create environments where those two things flourish until we change the template for what strong leadership looks like.

And this stuff will stick eventually. Trying to change the ingrained beliefs of a white, middle-aged, middle-class man who has always done things in a certain way and has no interest in having his worldview challenged may get you nowhere. But what about the guy in his thirties who's got a couple of young daughters and a pretty egalitarian set-up at home?

More nuance around what women in work, women in leadership and good leadership models across both genders look like will benefit everyone – whether you're a Beta bloke who's bored with all the willy-waving you have to do just to get a project signed off, or a young female graduate, who wishes the phrase 'willy-waving' had never been coined.

The vast majority of young men I have worked with, and are friends with, would hate to be accused of being a sexist dinosaur. Admittedly I work in a particularly liberal profession where being right-on is akin to godliness, but how many blokes in their twenties or thirties want to be That Guy at work? The guy female colleagues will avoid in the pub because he's said a few things that make you suspect he doesn't like women. The guy who can't work out why he's the only person on the team who's been sent to 'diversity training' three times in one year.

No one wants to be that guy. He's a throwback that shouldn't exist any more. And when we reach the point where more young men are being managed by smart, capable women and are just as in touch with their Beta side as their female colleagues, That Guy will become extinct. Which means we can all get on with our jobs, minus the pointless noise.

3.

SHOULDER PADS ARE BULLSHIT: ISN'T IT TIME WE REDEFINED WHAT A SUCCESSFUL WOMAN LOOKS LIKE?

When I was in my mid-twenties, I was offered a job I was potentially unqualified for. (At the time I assumed I was offered it because of some administrative error and decided to go along with it because I didn't want to stay where I was and . . . why not? Even now I'm not sure why I got it.) Not only did I not know what I was doing, I didn't even really want to be there. I think I thought that accepting the job would force me to become a different type of person – more professional and together. But, as I came to realise, there's nothing about having a panic attack in the second-floor loos on your first day to make you feel the opposite of professional and together.

Almost everyone on the team was older than me and, from what I could tell, a couple had turned my new job down because it was probably going to be a poisoned chalice – or, to use the vernacular, a total ball-ache. I had my first big team meeting about forty-eight hours after I'd started. It was the first time I'd had a team to manage, and I'd been told several times what an unenviable task I had on my hands. Budgets had been slashed, redundancies had been made, audience levels were sinking and several editors had been and gone in quick succession.

My team were crying out for a strong leader who'd turn them into a successful, motivated team working towards a coherent strategy and vision. And in the short term? They probably wanted a desk-thumping, shouty speech from me about how I was going to lead them to victory. And maybe the spectacle of me firing someone on the spot, just to show HOW VERY SERIOUS I was.

I knew I had to knock it out of the park. I had to make them realise I was the boss, that I was going to be their fearless leader, that I was going to take charge and sort stuff out and that I was to be obeyed at all times. In short, it was the most important meeting of my career to date. So I . . . fluffed it.

'This is a new start for everyone,' I began (for fun, I like to imagine that I sound exactly like the Queen at Christmas when I look back now and picture myself giving this speech). 'I know there's been a lot of upheaval in the last year but that's all about to change. [Sound of me unable to catch my breath.] I . . . uh . . . [face goes pink] . . . um . . . [tempo of foot-tapping increases dramatically] . . . aaaaand that's all. Thanks.'

My new team blinked in what certainly felt like total unison, then carried on as though it was a normal meeting, discussing their plans for that week's content (ostensibly pitching ideas to me, but in reality politely informing me of their plans, while I nodded and grinned manically).

I hadn't said anything horrendous, I hadn't lied, over-promised or misled them. I hadn't given away confidential information, pooed myself in fear or cried. I just hadn't done anything else either. And what they wanted from me was something. They wanted me to take the initiative. Or, at the very least, talk about how I was going to take the initiative at some point in the future.

As that meeting drew to a close, my team appeared to assume they were the victims of a cruel practical joke, but they weren't. They were stuck with me and, based on a one-hour meeting with absolutely no self-aggrandising speech, I wasn't up to the job. Because as much as I was confused about what success and successful looked like at that time, my team weren't. I wasn't it.

Because this was real life and not a film, there was no massive resolution. It kind of worked out okay in the end because some people left, and were replaced with a younger team I recruited, who saw me as the boss for that very reason. And I was older and more experienced than them, so of course I was making the decisions – authority is a pretty relative thing, as it turns out.

And when I stopped feeling as if my every move was being second-guessed, I relaxed into the job. I knew the answers to more questions than I didn't, and I stopped being the new girl. But that whole process would have happened in a third of the time if the expectation (mine and the team's) of what a boss should look like had been less rigid. As far as I and they were concerned, I was too young, too nice, too nervous, and I said, 'I don't know' seventy-five times a day. Therefore I was doomed to fail.

Success no longer means following a linear career path. It can be measured by Instagram followers, a banging Etsy store, or the blog you set up on your lunch breaks winning a bunch of awards. Yet our view of what a successful woman looks like remains incredibly rigid. We still expect successful women to dominate the room, the conversation, the meeting. We assume that the women we're hearing about bossing it in all industries must be Alpha because that's the way they're presented to us. Self-promotion comes far less easily to Beta women because we're not hardwired to push ourselves above everyone else, but even the most Beta entrepreneur will know how to compose the perfect rousing Instagram post about living her brand 24/7 or whatever, even if she cringes as she presses send. Because social media, the internet and the technology that have made it possible for us to follow such diverse and individual paths to success have removed so much of the nuance around how we're allowed to present ourselves. Even the most Beta woman can shout about herself in the most Alpha way when she's doing it from behind a screen. The result? The way success is viewed is becoming narrower, more homogeneous, not broader.

We tell young women that they need to become their own personal brands to succeed, to find their niche and learn how to market themselves. But are we teaching them how to lead for the future? How to collaborate, work with others and motivate people? (That is, how to be a good Beta boss.) Everyone is told to be disruptive, to tear up the norm and to lead from the front. But what if that model for success is at odds with your personality? What if disruption makes you anxious? What if you find leading from the front emotionally exhausting? How are you ever supposed to be the best version of yourself? And, crucially, why do we assume that disruption is always the best route to success?

Many of the accepted wisdoms I came out of school with – that vocational degrees aren't as valuable as humanities degrees, that three years at a Russell Group university will set you up with a job for life, that the internet is just a distraction – don't apply any more. So what skills do young women need to make it in the workplace now? And are they being taught them?

There's some pretty compelling evidence to suggest that careers advice to young women (and young people in general) is falling far short of where it needs to be. The 2015 *Scarred For Life?* report for the Young Women's Trust looked at, among other things, young people's experience of careers advice, and found that many of the young women and the organisations they spoke to were 'critical of the advice offered to those under sixteen, and consider that schools have been given an unrealistic challenge'. One government agency was cited in the report as observing, 'In schools we have found that the focus is on moving them [young women] onto anything rather than what they will do as a career.'

Similarly, the think-tank Fabian Society's 2014 report *Out of Sight* looked at what has happened to the fifty thousand or so NEET (Not in Education, Employment or Training) young people who have fallen out of the system. It found that careers advice is now the statutory responsibility of schools, and 'Unfortunately the careers advice in schools is systemically weak.' It points to Ofsted's 2013 report, which stated that just one in five secondary schools were giving their students effective careers advice. The report suggested that young people need careers advice that looks 'further ahead than the next course or year of learning. It is not enough for a young person to be participating in "something" between the ages of 16 and 18; even something for which they have a weak preference or interest. They must be working towards the time when they need to succeed in the competitive jobs market.'

The focus of these reports is young people who aren't necessarily going to university, but with the cost of tuition fees far outstripping what graduates can expect to earn, more young people will flounder for their next move once they've left full-time education. And when the focus seems to be to get young people onto a course – any course – where will they learn what it really takes to succeed in an ever-changing job market?

'The things young people have been told for the past twenty years or so are "Follow your dream, follow your passions. If you don't follow your passions you'll have an unhappy life,"' explains Tania Hummel, the HR consultant and executive coach we met earlier. 'So most of the things people have been told have turned out not to be true – "Go to university, get a degree, get a doctorate, get a great job." It's not happening. The world is changing too fast and the promises that were made are not being fulfilled.'

I take Tania's point – I left full-time education at the beginning of 2005, and everything I learnt seems hilariously obsolete now. But Tania believes that the uncertain nature of the world we're in may work in the Beta's favour. 'When the World Economic Forum wrote about the skills that people will need in the workplace in 2020 compared to 2015, they talked about critical thinking and emotional intelligence, and emotional intelligence was a totally new addition to that list.

'Because, actually, if you're looking at this volatile, complex, ambiguous world, where everything is so unpredictable, the only thing you can do is work on yourself and your own resilience to be able to cope and keep up and roll with the punches.'

Sociologist Dr Pamela Stone agrees that there's a generational shift in our attitudes towards success. 'When you swing away from the baby-boomer generation down through the millennials you do see a gradual moving away from a purely monetary, classic sense of achievement as being status and power and high salaries. You still have those old models in big hierarchical organisations employing lots of people – the IBMs, the big banks and so on. But that's all breaking up as we move to a gig economy [one where people are temporarily contracted to work for organisations for a short period, so essentially self-employed rather than in full-time work]. So when you move to an economy where you don't get jobs for life, there's no track, there's no ladder to climb, there's no natural hierarchy. So it's not surprising to me as a sociologist that millennials are modifying what they call success, because there's no way for them of achieving success according to the old model.'

Writing for Fast Company, LinkedIn's Eddie Vivas believes that the so-called gig economy will soon become . . . life. 'We're about to see more power shift away from companies and into job seekers' hands as technology makes it easier than ever to find or change jobs,' he explains. 'The rise of gig-economy players, like Uber, Lyft and Upwork, is just the latest evidence of a trend that's set to continue, with technology empowering people to take more direct control of their careers and livelihoods – even if the world that it ultimately creates isn't something we'll still call the "gig economy", as though it's something distinct from the job market overall. Because, increasingly, it won't be.'

The Deloitte Global Human Capital Trends report for

2016 found that 42 per cent of US executives expected to use more contingent workers (freelancers, or giggers, if you will) in the next three to five years, and that a third of American workers are freelancers, with that set to increase to 40 per cent by 2020.

The report pointed out that many companies are moving away from a hierarchical organisational structure towards a model where teams come together to tackle a specific project before disbanding again. Which means employers are increasingly looking for freelancers who can demonstrate strong project management and team-working skills.

Plenty of the skill associated with this evolving economy will make easy reading for most Betas – emotional intelligence, the ability to work with different types of people, and to be flexible and pragmatic are classic Beta traits. But in an economy where we're increasingly likely to be working for ourselves and placing increasing value on our personal brand and our ability to self-promote, are we going to become a world of Betas in Alpha clothing?

Maybe so. The report also – unsurprisingly – identifies networking as a key skill to embrace in the gig economy. And Susan Chritton, an executive career coach, also identifies development of your personal brand as one of the key and unavoidable skills required to thrive in the gig economy. 'Having a strong personal brand will serve you well in the gig economy,' she explains, in *Personal Branding for Dummies*. 'Instead of hoping that someone notices you and offers you steady, long-term employment, you must be prepared to take your personal brand on the road and leverage your skills.'

Now, I know plenty of Betas who are also excellent

networkers, but I'm not sure I'd count myself among them. I can do it if I have to, but I have to psych myself up and pretty much pretend to be a different person to resist the almost overwhelming urge to stand in the corner and shove canapés into my mouth until I'm allowed to go home. Basically, I have to be a Beta in Alpha clothing. How very gig economy of me.

But the 'in Alpha clothing' bit is crucial – I still have to play dress up because success still only looks one way. Our world is constantly and quickly changing, yet certain values remain at a premium. And most of us learn that quickly – which is why the way people use social media has almost instinctively shifted in line with this new economy.

Have a quick flick through your Instagram and check out #buildingmyempire: apart from all the motivational memes, it's filled with snapshots of people's lives that demonstrate just how much they're 'bossing it', 'smashing it' or 'nailing it' (pick your favourite). Not shown: when they spent a week staring at a wall because they couldn't work out what to do next, or took on some personal brand unfriendly data-entry work to pay that month's rent, or how much of their new business venture is being funded by their parents. Why don't we see those bits too? Because they don't fit with the tale we're trying to tell.

We're increasingly taught to create a narrative around our careers and our (back to that phrase again) personal brands. You know the adversity-story thing they always do on *The X Factor*? In the last few weeks of the competition, as things start to hot up, they'll introduce a narrative around each of the remaining contestants. The detail is always slightly different, but the gist is the same: something bad happened to them in the past that makes this particular contestant's Personal Journey to the finals more poignant than those of the others. Then they'll talk about How Far They've Come, before cutting to a family member, who confirms that said contestant has indeed Come Far. Finally, the video will cut back to the contestant, who will say, 'This has been a dream come true for me. It's been the journey of a lifetime. I don't know what I'll do if I go home tonight,' before bursting into tears. Rinse and repeat.

There's little variation on this theme, although I remember one year watching a grown man sobbing to camera because he couldn't bear the thought of going back to putting up wedding marquees for a living.

So why do it?

Because we root for people who have a clear story – beat the odds, fight against adversity and win – whether that's presented in a video clip before one goes on stage to belt out a cover version of 'If I Can Turn Back Time', or through a series of motivational Instagram memes. Whether your business is building or blogging, if people root for you and relate to you, they're more likely to support your endeavour.

And all this might feel inauthentic, or like a distraction from the bigger picture or a bit . . . boasty? Immodest? . . . but there's no escaping it. And when everyone else is shouting loudly about their achievements, keeping quiet about yours doesn't make you modest or discreet. It means no one will ever hear about them.

But how do you have any semblance of work/life balance when your work revolves around your personal brand? Emma Gannon has made a career out of her personal brand – and with a blog, book (*Ctrl Alt Delete: How I*

Grew Up Online) and podcast of the same name, she's a poster-child for how success can look in the Noughties. I'd say she was Alpha because her career is so closely tied to who she is. And, given that her personal brand is her career, I'd say, based on what I see on social media, she's never not working. But is that an illusion?

'It definitely looks like I do more work than I am doing in the evenings, because it comes very easily to me now,' she admits. 'I'll do a blog page in half an hour and spend the rest of the evening with my boyfriend. But it probably looks like I've spent the whole night doing something.'

And it's that filter through which we view other people's lives that can alter our perception of what success looks like. Emma certainly works hard, but is the sixteen-year-old girl who follows her and dreams of a similar career getting a true version of her life?

'It's curated. You're not lying but you are leaving stuff out. So you're always telling the truth. I'm presenting the truth at all times, but it's like a sliver of everything. And I do genuinely believe that we have an offline and an online identity now.'

I'm not a sixteen-year-old girl and I should certainly know better, but the issue I've had when comparing myself to colleagues and other women in my industry is that I take the filtered snapshots of their lives as a statement of fact – which means my own work ethic, enthusiasm and, indeed, life come up wanting (and again, yes, I should know better). It makes me feel inadequate and it makes my life seem banal and suburban by comparison. Far from inspiring me, it leaves me feeling that I'm not living my life in the right way. Because, for me, that's another element of what being a successful Alpha woman looks like: being always on, always focused, always thinking about work, 24/7. In my head, this (fictional) success story never wastes twenty minutes gazing out of the window, daydreaming about what she'd wear to collect her Oscar for best screenplay. Ahem.

It takes Emma to remind me that no one's living their role 24/7, even if it appears they are. 'How can you be Alpha and be a human being? Because you can't be Alpha all the time. We're all vulnerable. Like I'm not going to be an Alpha if I go to a grandparent's funeral. You just can't be.'

Emma thinks those days of presenting ourselves as always-on superwomen are over and we're looking for more authenticity in our role models. 'I don't think we respond to Alpha women as much as we used to, maybe. I don't know. I just know that, as a twenty-something, I don't look up to and idolise a career woman who shuts herself off from being authentic. We're used to bloggers and YouTubers and the like who are talking about their depression, or what medication they're on, or how they feel when someone they know has died. We're used to seeing human beings 360, so when you're presented with a 2-D cut-out of someone who's really successful it's like "Well, I can't connect with you."'

'Authenticity' is a word I've been hearing a lot – authenticity is apparently why some YouTube vloggers have reached the stratospheric levels of fame among teenage audiences previously only enjoyed by boy bands. And lack of authenticity is a charge that gets levelled at any person, or brand, who can't connect with their audience. When then Labour leader Ed Miliband was lampooned after being photographed eating a bacon sandwich in the run-up to the 2015 election, it was because no one believed he really *meant* to eat it. Eating a sandwich was seen as a cynical (and failed) stunt and became an emblem of his failure to connect with voters. You may have thought it was impossible to eat a bacon sandwich inauthentically, but you'd be wrong.

Yet when Ed Balls – another Labour politician who inauspiciously lost his job at the 2015 election – agreed to be a contestant on *Strictly Come Dancing*, a gig with arguably more potential for public humiliation than eating a pork-based breakfast staple when there are cameras around, he went from unpopular ex-politician to national treasure. Why? Because he came across as completely authentic. He was a middle-aged man in the aftermath of an enforced career change, trying something new, often failing, but trying nonetheless.

Politicians, individuals and brands know that they need to appear authentic to connect with their audiences, but what they are slower to realise is that you can't stage-manage human connection. 'Being yourself' only works as a selling point if you're not trying. The minute it becomes a conscious effort, you're putting on an act. And people aren't stupid: they notice.

It's the same when you're leading a team. 'Your greatest impact as a person and as a leader is authenticity,' agrees Eddie Erlandson. 'You can't fake it, and if you're a non-Alpha, and you're working around Alphas you may need to adapt your style at times to be effective with Alphas, but it doesn't mean you change.'

Erlandson believes that good leadership is less about Alpha and Beta, and more about specific personality traits – some people are more fine-tuned for it than others. 'I think the good leader is the one that people will follow. If people are not following, and you are not able to generate productivity and output and creativity then you are missing the mark on leadership. The really good leader, in my opinion, is the conscious leader, the one who is self-aware, who is aware of other people, who can basically adapt on the fly to have healthy influence and create healthy accountability.'

Take this description of working for Jeff Bezos, chairman and CEO of Amazon by Manfred Kets de Vries, a clinical professor of leadership development and organisational change at INSEAD, writing on the INSEAD website: 'Working for Bezos is quite a challenge. He is a typical Alpha male: hardheaded, task-oriented and extremely opinionated. He is known to get very upset when things do not go his way, and living up to his excessively high standards can feel like a mission impossible.

'The more pressure Bezos feels to perform, the more his leadership style transforms from being constructive and challenging to intimidating and even abusive. He is known for outbursts of anger when things don't go his way – a consequence of his total commitment to customer service – and for making demoralising statements like, "Why are you wasting my life?", "I'm sorry, did I take my stupid pills today?" or "This document was clearly written by the B team. Can someone get me the A team document?"

'In his dynamic, metrics-driven corporate culture, there is little time for soft talk. He is even known to walk away from meetings if people do not get to the point quickly. Faced with this Alpha-male behaviour, people who work for him do so in constant fear. While this Darwinian-like, performance-based culture reaps benefits for Amazon's customers, it comes at the price of a devalued and demoralised workforce.'

Kets de Vries points out that although Alpha leaders often possess a huge amount of drive and passion, it can be accompanied by a fatal flaw – narcissism means they are often unable to recognise their own limits, so when the pressure on them increases, their leadership style can go from constructive and challenging to intimidating and even abusive. 'Not surprisingly given their dysfunctional behaviour,' he concludes, 'companies run by destructive Alphas can easily go down the drain.'

And when it does go wrong? It's time for a change of management style, as Tania Hummel explains: 'For some reason it would appear that most companies hire women when things are going wrong and they hire men when things are going right. I would speculate that this is because women would be more likely to bring people together, to be a reassuring presence and to be more cautious when times are difficult.'

Actual success is far more difficult to quantify than we pretend, but if you're looking for it from a bloke in a suit shouting in a boardroom, you might be looking in the wrong place.

In the Introduction, I described what I imagine when I think about Alpha Woman as a person – she's successful and perhaps a little intimidating, yes, but she's still human. We can all identify her because we've all worked with someone like her.

But imagine if you had to personify female success itself: what would that look like? Again, she's probably tall, white, middle class, university-educated, perfectly dressed, well-groomed and articulate. She's also decisive, focused and driven. Are her team scared of her and her peers in awe of her? Is she always prepared, never caught out, unafraid of confrontation and never without her blow-dry?

Of course she is. She's Alpha Woman, and she's nowhere near as much fun at parties as the Cool Girl identified by Gillian Flynn's *Gone Girl*, described perfectly by protagonist Amy:

> Men always say that as the defining compliment, don't they? She's a cool girl. Being the Cool Girl means I am a hot, brilliant, funny woman who adores football, poker, dirty jokes, and burping, who plays video games, drinks cheap beer, loves threesomes and anal sex, and jams hot dogs and hamburgers into her mouth like she's hosting the world's biggest culinary gang bang while somehow maintaining a size 2, because Cool Girls are above all hot. Hot and understanding. Cool Girls never get angry; they only smile in a chagrined, loving manner and let their men do whatever they want. Go ahead, shit on me, I don't mind, I'm the Cool Girl.

But the point is, Cool Girl isn't real, as Amy explains: 'Men actually think this girl exists. Maybe they're fooled because so many women are willing to pretend to be this girl.'

And it's the same thing here: Alpha Woman – as in the embodiment of what we see female success to be – is just as much a work of fiction. Most of us could pretend to be her if we really wanted to – a shameless deployment of Instagram, a healthy dose of narcissism and a little creative licence will do it. But it isn't real and it isn't what success is. Success is whatever gets you out of bed and into work in the morning – whether that's a creative passion, the desire to see the job through or just the knowledge that you'll pay your rent this month. You haven't failed if you haven't met a series of arbitrary requirements that have no bearing on your actual life, and the very fact that we're telling ourselves that we have, day in day out, is total nonsense.

So let's lift the curtain and start giving ourselves a pat on the back for our actual success and stop thinking about our perceived failures. (Got that very boring PowerPoint done for your boss? Hurrah, give yourself a pat on the back and bask in the warm glow you get only when you complete a task well and on deadline. Exceeded expectations in all sections of your annual review this year? Make yourself a cup of tea and text your mum to celebrate! You deserve it!)

Success is about what we have done and what we can do. It's about achievements. It's not about image and it's not about how many things you can cram into every given day. If you want to see what successful looks like, get off social media and look in the mirror.

4.

I remember the first time I was interviewed for a Saturday job. I was sixteen and had seen an advert in the paper that said the picture-framers around the corner from my parents' house in Harrow wanted someone who could help out on a Saturday. I assumed it would involve ringing stuff up on the cash register, finding people's orders, that sort of thing. It quickly transpired that they were after something a bit more involved – someone who could advise clients on mountings and frames for their pictures. They'd need to demonstrate that they had 'an eye'. Suffice to say, I don't. I harbour no secret desire to become an artist. Nor do I believe I'd make a great interior designer in another life. I could work out a 20 per cent sale discount on a watercolour from a local artist and ring it through the till, no problem. But advise on the best border to go with a specific frame? Absolutely not.

So, over the course of a twenty-minute interview, the job went from something I could do in a heartbeat to wildly out of my comfort zone. For the first time I experienced what's now an all too familiar feeling: that I was a fraud who really shouldn't be there. Or, at least, I'd become a fraud if I were to maintain the fiction that I was a competent person who knew what they were doing (albeit within the very specific realms of framing mediocre watercolours for the residents of Harrow).

I said as much to the manager of the shop. (Actually, I whispered it, complete with a stutter and a red-hot face, and I didn't mention the mediocre part.) He looked a little confused, then disappointed, and said, 'I really don't understand you. You've instantly gone from seeming incredibly confident and competent to really nervous and young.' I think what he was getting at was . . . Couldn't I have just faked it? I didn't know what I was doing, but I'd have worked it out eventually, and I certainly wouldn't have done an absolutely horrible job. But, actually, at that first interview I developed a pattern that has followed me round for most of my working life. When I know that I know something, I'm fine. But the minute I'm unsure, or I think someone else knows more than I do, I'm plagued with self-doubt. With that Saturday job, the minute I realised there would be someone else out there who would do a better job than me, I didn't want it. Because what I hadn't worked out, aged sixteen, is that most people are faking it a lot of the time – and some people are faking it all of the time. No one is the perfect fit for the job they're in, knows what they're doing all of the time, or feels comfortable in every situation. The difference between an Alpha and a Beta is that an Alpha would never not fake it.

But working that one out – and this is no exaggeration – has been one of the most important lessons of my career to date. For one thing, it meant I stopped looking like a terrified teenager every time I was asked something I didn't understand. 'Fake it till you make it' is the philosophy of one of my favourite ever bosses (a true Alpha, in case you're wondering). And although I still think pretending to be someone you're not for great swathes of time is the stuff of nightmares, there's something strangely liberating about the discovery that everyone is putting it on, and that you're basically operating in a carefully constructed skit. It's like imagining the audience members of your public-speaking engagement are all naked – but for life.

There are two dangers. The first, of course, comes when we forget that everyone else is faking it, and when we start to take all the posturing seriously and try to match up to it. Second, faking self-confidence in a meeting when you're nervous is a very different proposition from being totally inauthentic all of the time. The latter – I believe – can make us really very unhappy. But more on that later.

While I may have failed in my first attempt at faking it, back in 1999, I'm a veritable pro now, in that, like most of you, I'll probably fake it several times a week. With a lightly filtered Instagram post cropping out the dirty plates or pile of boxes in the background. Or a tweet about a huge work achievement without mentioning that getting said work achievement out of the door nearly made me cry from tiredness and anxiety. Life is never easy or effort-less, and it's probably not meant to be, so why do we continue to propagate the myth that we're having a great time, even when we've got period pains, a cold and we're four days late paying our rent?

The self-discrepancy theory was developed by E. Tory Higgins in 1987 (before Instagram was barely a glimmer in someone's eye), and it looks at the discrepancy between our different selves. Our actual self – who we actually are, our ideal self – the person we want to be, and our ought self, which is our understanding of what others want us to be. The self-discrepancy theory looks at what happens when our ideal and ought selves don't match up with our actual self. In short, it results in psychological and emotional turmoil. When we don't match up with our ideal self we feel disappointed, sad or despondent because we aren't the version of our self we want to be. When we don't match up with our ought self we feel agitated, guilty, distressed and anxious because we feel as if we have violated some perceived standard we should be living up to.

So, my ideal self may be a version of me who organises my outfits for the week and makes lunches on a Sunday night (instead of spending all my money in Pret), and has a handbag that isn't covered with ink and full of fluff-covered cashew nuts. I'd probably go to the gym more often, have shinier hair and drink less too. These are all achievable things that I feel better about when I achieve them but don't cause me particular levels of anxiety when I can't.

My ought self is someone who shows impeccable judgement, makes decisions quickly and brilliantly, is slightly scary but also well respected. She is fine with confrontation and happy to tell people what they don't want to hear. She never puts being liked above getting the job done. These are all things I think I should do, and ways I think I should be, and I feel guilty and anxious when I don't live up to them. And, of course, I don't live up to them because they're not who I actually am. They're benchmarks of a standard I feel I should live up to.

Social psychologist Ben Voyer also believes we use social media to try to reconcile these different senses of self – further complicating what actually makes it onto our social-media output: 'Individuals are consistently torn between their actual, desired and ought selves, and use social media to try to reconcile these – or sometimes to construct what they think would be the best possible "ideal self".'

And let's not forget that we're naturally performative creatures – the act of playing a part is one that comes naturally to us, and long predates Twitter and Facebook. 'The American sociologist Erving Goffman introduced in the 1950s a difference between what he called a "public self" and a "private self",' explains Professor Voyer. 'The private self is a self that we keep for ourselves, and maybe close others and relatives. The public self is a self that we manage and shape so that it conforms to what we want others to think we are. Goffman's approach is known as a "dramaturgical approach," meaning that he suggests that individuals are "actors" of their own lives. We now increasingly "stage" our lives online.'

But what happens when we're constantly playing a role in our own lives? Social media is regularly blamed for rising levels of anxiety and depression – and maybe this is why. We exist in a world where we're trying to live up to a perceived standard set by whomever we happen to follow on social media. Meanwhile we're constantly pushing an 'ideal' version of ourselves out there, which means that, at the same time, we're probably distorting the standard by which other people feel they should be living their lives.

If you've ever felt a twinge of jealousy, FOMO, or indeed guilt at someone else's perfectly curated Instagram post, a bit sad about your jacket-potato dinner because it looks like crap, even with the Clarendon filter, or faked an early-morning gym-class post (disclaimer: I've done all of the above), you'll know what I'm talking about.

Writer Daisy Buchanan agrees that the way we communicate on social media is fuelling a pursuit of perfection we'll never live up to. 'We cannot underestimate how much social media has changed things and how the meaning of perfect has changed, and perfect has become impossible; but we're still doing it, we're still flinging ourselves into the fray. "Goals" has become the hashtag of the decade; and it's become meaningless because we never stop to celebrate, it's always – what's the next goal?'

Ah #goals. Work #goals, life #goals, friendship #goals – all new arbitrary benchmarks to set ourselves based on someone else's (probably fairly inaccurate) social-media output to make ourselves feel guilty about something else we haven't done.

And it's making us feel bad. Anxiety and depression among young women are on the rise: a 2016 NHS study found that 12.6 per cent of women aged 16–24 screen positive for post-traumatic stress disorder; 26 per cent of women of the same age had anxiety, depression, panic disorders, phobias or obsessive compulsive disorder. Sally McManus, the lead researcher on the survey, said at the time that social media was a likely factor: 'This is the age of social-media ubiquity. This is the context that young women are coming into and it warrants further research.'

Another study by the University of Copenhagen suggests that too much Facebook browsing at Christmas specifically can make you miserable – because seeing other people's apparently perfect families can have that effect. Researchers warn of a 'deterioration of mood' from spending too long looking at other people's social-media stories, sparked by 'unrealistic social expectations'.

And the more our working lives become intertwined with the rest of our lives, the harder it is to resist the feeling that we're not quite nailing it at work. That we're not pulling enough late nights, not networking right, that our desks don't pass the Instagram test. (Incidentally, mine very much does not. Last year I discovered a mouse colony living in the empty cardboard boxes, with the bag of sunflower seeds and old gym towel under my desk. Turns out that the strange smell that had been emanating from my corner of the office was mouse urine. I did not put *this* on social media.)

I only realised how much I marked my own success by external factors rather than what I'm actually achieving at work when I was bemoaning my relative lack of success to my boyfriend. He asked me how my success was measured by my boss, and by the company I work for. By any measure I was achieving what I needed to, but because I didn't think I 'looked' or 'acted' like the right sort of success, I felt a failure.

Ironically, the bigger the gap between our actual self and our ought self, the less likely we are to achieve anything. Studies show that those with high levels of actual–ought discrepancy show the highest levels of procrastination.

When you think about it, that makes sense. Our ideal self is focused on achievement and successful goal pursuit; our ought self is about avoiding harm and not doing something bad. When our attitude to other people's social-media output starts to feed into our ought self, the entire interaction becomes negative, based on guilt and anxiety.

'The way we are is influenced by millions of other fake selves that we interact with constantly,' agrees Daisy. 'Sometimes I think I can type faster than I can articulate something. I never say, "Um, well, you know . . ." on Twitter whereas that makes up most of my actual conversation.'

So what's the answer? And if the life advice to live by is always to present a true version of yourself on social media, is that even possible?

For writer Laura Jane Williams, who wrote a personal memoir called *Becoming*, authenticity in her social-media output is important. 'The biggest compliment someone can pay me is when they say, "I follow you on Instagram and you're exactly how I thought you'd be in real life. I pride myself on that. I feel like a very responsible social-media user."'

But when Laura was diagnosed with depression and anxiety, shortly before the release of her second book, she discovered just how quickly and easily people make assumptions about you based on your output at any given moment: 'I'd released an e-book the year before last called *The Book of the Brave* . . . and this person said to me, "I just never thought you'd get depression after writing something like that."

'I thought, Oh, my God, this person thinks I sold a mistruth when I wrote this book about being brave and bold. And actually that was so, so true in that moment, and now my moment is raw and sad and blue and I'm documenting that in a different way and it's all about who I am, but you can't communicate those things all at once in what is essentially a two-dimensional medium.'

Because human beings are complex and complicated, when we present ourselves as one thing (Happy! Successful! Bored! Lonely!), which may be completely true in that moment, we forget that although we may have moved on to something else in the next instant, the snapshot we presented is what other people will see and remember. People – naturally – make assumptions about each other based on the information they have and, with the best will in the world, a ten-minute conversation face-to-face still reveals more about our true selves than a social-media post ever could. It's not that we're faking it or being fake online, it's just that it's only part of the story. Yet it's often the only part of the story we see.

Blogger and writer Emma Gannon believes that you can't fake the authenticity of someone who is truly happy in their skin, no matter how many filters you use. 'I believe in faking it until you're making it. I think when you get more relaxed, genuinely happy in yourself and in your career, there's no need to fake it any more. I've seen that in myself, and I've seen it in people I admire.'

But I still feel there are huge, crashing limits to how authentic anyone can be online because it's still a controlled image. It's who we want to be in that moment, not who we are.

And we can't even necessarily make the distinction ourselves. Studies show that we don't always have the self-awareness to know when we're posting a photo for validation rather than just for fun (although, seriously, when was the last time you posted anything and could convince yourself it was 'just for fun' and not for the associated validation?). Which makes it difficult to gauge how much we rely on the validation we receive from likes, retweets, comments and posts to give us a sense of self. How often do you stop to consider your motivation before posting a picture on Instagram or sending a Snapchat?

Take, for example, the evolution of the selfie. I've never liked photos of myself because, apart from anything else, they don't represent how I see myself in the mirror. A static image is obviously different from a moving one, and in the mirror my face is reversed. But this is how I see myself, and when I discover that other people see me differently, it makes me uncomfortable. But I'm much happier with a picture I've taken on my phone into a mirror. Why? Because it comes closer to representing how I think I look (never mind that this is further away from how I actually look – 'actually' isn't the point). Selfies give us a unique opportunity to control our image – and if these heavily edited, flatteringly posed, lit and filtered pictures are the only version of ourselves that people see, then that becomes what we look like. To our followers, that is reality.

Which actually feeds into another school of thought: maybe the idea that the people who appear the most successful, who have the most perfectly created lives *are* the most successful, is an illusion. Maybe it's the exact opposite: that those who are shouting the loudest may be faking it most. I asked Daisy Buchanan what she thought of people who posted about their early-morning gym classes before heading off to their high-powered jobs. (For some reason, it's this particular combination that really gets to me – I could probably, at a push, get up and go to the gym super-early if I had to. I could do a full day in the office, then an event in the evening, but I've never been together enough to do all three in one day. Apart from anything else, I wouldn't remember to pack enough pairs of pants.)

As Daisy points out, intention with that sort of online posturing is crucial. 'So much depends on attitude. If I got up at 4 a.m. to go to the gym, but did so because I was sad and I felt insecure about my body, and I found it a very difficult experience, then that would feel like quite a Beta thing to do.'

And, of course, we can never know someone's true intention or the full story behind how someone chooses to present themselves online. And, as we've already seen, the reasons behind why someone chooses to behave in a certain way on social media are far too complex to second-guess. The early-morning spinning-class picture could represent a massive sense of achievement, a massive feeling of stress, or a torn hamstring, we just don't know.

A friend and I were recently discussing a party she had gone to and I had skipped in favour of a night in the local pub. The party looked insanely cool and hipstery on Instagram, and played a massive part in my Sunday morning, guilty-hung-over FOMO. ('What's the point of getting trashed and having a hangover if you're not at a party like that?' was my general thinking.)

It turned out the party was horrible: the drinks were too expensive, everyone was really obnoxious, and they all fell out, which meant groups of people were huddled in various corners of the room, crying or throwing vitriolic glances at each other. Of course, I wouldn't have known this because, to give the impression that they were HAVING A GREAT TIME, everyone came together for the obligatory group selfies halfway through the night, then skulked back to their respective corners. I know, mental.

Basically, the only authenticity or truth you can get from

most people's social-media output is how much time and energy they're willing to put into curating it.

But what if you have no social-media output? Is that the mark of an ultimate Alpha?

Or put it this way: a lot of what I imagine to be my most Beta traits probably stem from my adjusting my behaviour or decision-making to keep other people happy – to ensure they like me. So: what's the difference between me taking on work that probably isn't mine to keep the peace and avoid confrontation, and sharing or liking a cringy aphorism on Instagram posted by someone you admire? And what's the difference between a self-deprecating 'Aren't I scatty?' Facebook post and me telling a self-deprecating 'Aren't I scatty?' story in real life – when I'll probably exaggerate my own stupidity and ignore the fact that 80 per cent of the time I'm not particularly scatty at all?

I always think a true Alpha IRL is someone who ploughs their own furrow, irrespective of other people's opinions (they rarely ask for them). Surely in Social Media Land, this becomes someone who doesn't think twice about retweets, comments or their social reach. Perhaps opting out of all media where you're expected to project a version of yourself to other people for scrutiny, judgement and approval (because, at its heart, that's what the majority of social-media interaction is) is the truest sign there is of someone who is genuinely comfortable in their own skin and totally self-possessed. Actually, that's a level of high Alpha-ness I could genuinely aspire to.

'I've definitely become more independent in how I think about things and how I conduct myself, which was kind of the point,' explains Rachel, a thirty-four-year-old teacher, who deleted her Instagram, Facebook and Twitter accounts when she realised just how much they were impacting on her decisions and thought patterns. 'Instagram was the worst, because it was affecting what I wore, the decisions I made about which parties to go to, the kind of friends I hung out with.

'I've always prided myself on being a really independent thinker, but there's such a sheep-like quality to how we behave on social media that even when someone is posting something that's meant to demonstrate how quirky or individual they are, it's really just a reflection of what they think other quirky or individual people are doing.'

And now she's gone social-media cold turkey? 'It's that massive cliché but I definitely feel more present in the moment. I hadn't realised how much I'd stopped making decisions about what I wanted based on what was happening in my actual life as opposed to my virtual world. I'm sure some people can separate out the two consciously, but I don't think I'm one of them.'

The focus might be on Facebook when it comes to how we disseminate and share news, and distinguish fact from fiction, but I really believe that the insidious ways in which Instagram now influences our behaviour are becoming far more ingrained – and sinister because we don't realise it's happening.

Look at the beauty industry: sales for contouring kits, foundations and illuminators designed to give you the perfect selfie-ready face have shot up in the last few years, and while it was estimated that in the UK we took 1.2 billion selfies in 2014, the earned media value (EMV) for brands and influencers across different platforms found the EMV for Instagram had increased more than nine-fold from 2014 to 2015, according to digital marketers Tribe Dynamics. This is compared to 26 per cent for blogs.

I think the specific problem with Instagram is that compared to, say, Facebook, which your mum is on, posting twenty-three pictures from your nan's seventy-fifth birthday party, it is designed to promote a snapshot or a single moment. Even if that moment is true for just the next thirty seconds, it quickly becomes part of your past – but for the person looking at it, liking it, chewing their lip in anxiety because they're not having as much fun or aren't as thin, it's the present.

When Essena O'Neill, an Australian teenager with half a million Instagram followers, loudly announced in 2015 that she was quitting Instagram, she described the platform as 'contrived perfection made to get attention'. 'I remember I obsessively checked the like count for a full week since uploading it,' she wrote at the time, on her first ever post. 'It got five likes. This was when I was so hungry for social-media validation . . . Now marks the day I quit all social media and focus on real-life projects.'

But it's not just teenagers, it's all of us. It's lawyers, doctors, engineers in their twenties, thirties, forties and beyond. We're all buying into it and we're all left wanting. And how we are at work – how successful, organised, passionate – has become as big a part of that fiction as how we look in a bikini or how many squats we managed that day.

I mean, I'm not sure if, in the twenty-first century Western world, being truly comfortable with your sense of self, relationships and environment is even possible. But if it is, isn't that a true Alpha Nirvana we could all work towards? And if that is the case, surely any concern about how you're projecting yourself to others (which is 95 per cent of most people's social-media output) is a total anathema.

Working out that everyone is faking it was one of the best things I've ever done. Learning to stop faking it is something I'm still working on. Authenticity – the buzzword *du jour* – should be easy. Just be yourself, right? But the reality is, it's harder than ever.

I wrote this book to try to work out if and articulate how you can be just as successful in the workplace if you're a Beta woman as you could be as an Alpha woman. And to do that we have to look at the bars against which we all measure ourselves. Some are the standards set by our employers or potential employers, but many are the standards we set for ourselves and others. And as much as social media is, on the face of it, a place to celebrate individuality, most of us are still marching to a fairly homogeneous tune in terms of how we measure and celebrate female success.

And that is why Betas need to write their own tune. We could all spend years on Instagram, ruminating on other people's apparent success and how we fall short in comparison. But focusing on what success looks like for us IRL, and striving for it, sounds far more satisfying and fruitful to me.

5.

Every negative moment in my career has one common
thread: an overriding belief that I don't belong in that role,
that I'm not good enough and never should have been given
the job in the first place. As part of my first job, for that
small agency in south London, I ended up covering a mater-
nity leave after someone else had dropped out suddenly. It
was a big promotion to editor, but in reality I'd been doing
the job unofficially for months without a problem. But
that was because I knew I was helping out as a favour,
rather than doing the job for real, which meant I was happy
and confident that I was doing well. The minute I was
given the editing job that changed.

It was a tricky gig, involving lots of late nights, constant
pressure and difficult clients, who wanted constant assur-
ance that they were getting value for money. They wanted
to know they were getting a proper editor, not an editorial
assistant who'd been given a new job title.

And that was the problem. The more the pressure was
piled on, and the harder it got, the more I started to agree
with their assessment that I was absolutely useless.
Producing the magazine was the easy part – we had a
fantastic team and everyone knew what they were doing
– but dealing with the client was a whole other ball game.

Yes, they were demanding, but so were most clients, and

they were by no means impossible. And, anyway, I'd worked with them for years before that without incident. But I became so convinced of and consumed by my own ineptitude that every change they wanted to make felt like a criticism of me personally. And every time they challenged me (in hindsight they were trying to get the measure of me) I crumbled. It wasn't that I couldn't do or wasn't doing the job, it was that my belief that I was the wrong person to be there became so overwhelming that it was all I let other people see.

It was almost like the opposite of 'Fake it till you make it.' I couldn't project any measure of confidence or competence lest people get the wrong impression of me. If I acted like I didn't know what I was doing, at least people would be pleasantly surprised if I came good. And if I messed up? At least I could say, 'I told you so.'

I've made a conscious effort to change how I project myself as I've got older. (I don't think I've got it nailed: I still frequently feel like the least competent, least serious and least grown-up person in the room, and it probably shows.) And it's not necessarily that I've got better at hiding it when I'm terrified or out of my depth. It's more that I've realised that messing up, getting things wrong and not knowing the answers are a fact of life, not a mark of incompetence. I've become less scared of failure, which has made the thought of failing less scary. And, crucially, I've stopped thinking that making a mistake or not knowing something automatically means I shouldn't be doing my job or that I'm a fraud. It's called Impostor Syndrome and we all get it (although the jury is out on whether women get it more than men). If you're a Beta woman in the workplace, I'm guessing it has had a marked impact on your career.

Impostor Syndrome was first recognised in 1978 by Georgia State University when academics realised that successful women had high levels of self-doubt. It can be defined as 'a psychological phenomenon in which people are unable to internalise their accomplishments. Despite external evidence of their competence, those with the syndrome remain convinced that they are frauds and do not deserve the success they have achieved.' So that'll be me, then.

Naomi, thirty-three, is a project manager in the construction industry. In her experience, Impostor Syndrome is a uniquely female phenomenon, which she particularly noted working in her male-dominated industry. 'I have rarely met a man at work who struggles with confidence or a sense of belonging, but I have met a lot of women who do. We feel out of place in an environment that is not designed for us, or led by us. Having worked in construction for six years I have seen how intimidating male-dominated environments can be. Men and women are also motivated differently, and I think we seek external praise more often than men do.'

It's certainly something she's experienced: 'Despite years of project-management experience, and proven delivery, I struggle to believe that I am the right person for a job. I often fear that I'm about to be tapped on the shoulder and told, "it's okay. We know you don't know anything. You can go home now!" And this is despite getting nothing but positive feedback in every job I've ever had.'

Now, I'm not a perfectionist in the classic sense. My

approach to most projects could charitably be described as having a 'helicopter view' – I'm great with big ideas, but get a little bored when it comes to the detail and final execution. I'm also generally happy to let smaller stuff go, even if it's not quite right – I'd always rather get it done than get it perfect. But that's okay – I try to work with people who are more detail-oriented and, between us, we tend to get the job done. But I do set insanely high demands on my own time – the number of things I want to get done in any given day is always a stretch target, and I always feel like I'm a disaster when, inevitably, I don't get through everything on my to-do list. I feel that, if I'm not constantly busy and constantly productive, I'm failing. I only have two settings: total success or total failure. Which means, if I'm not 100 per cent nailing it (and, let's face it, who's doing that all of the time?), I feel as if I shouldn't be there.

I'm not alone: Sheryl Sandberg, Facebook's COO, has said, 'There are still days when I wake up feeling like a fraud, not sure I should be where I am.' Actress and UN ambassador Emma Watson and actress Kate Winslet have admitted to suffering from Impostor Syndrome, while writer Maya Angelou once said, 'I have written eleven books, but each time I think, Uh-oh, they're going to find out now.' If those women are getting Impostor Syndrome, then it's probably okay if you or I are too.

The problem with Impostor Syndrome is that it doesn't push us to be better. Instead it makes us crave anonymity. A study by Ghent University has found that, rather than working harder to prove their abilities, sufferers bury themselves in their tasks and avoid extra responsibilities, becoming trapped in an 'impostor cycle'.

When I look back to that job where I was suddenly made editor, this resonates. It wasn't that I simply felt I didn't deserve to be there, it was that the Impostor Syndrome fed on itself, making me smaller, more cautious and more timid. Every day became about survival, not getting found out, rather than doing more, or doing things better. It wasn't about winning praise, accolades or awards or doing a good job. It was about keeping my head down and not being found out for the fraud I felt like.

Some studies demonstrate that Impostor Syndrome increases when women begin comparing themselves to their high-achieving female colleagues. In a 2013 study US sociologists Jessica Collett and Jade Avelis investigated why so many female academics ended up 'downshifting' – switching path from a high-status tenured post to something less ambitious. Impostorism was to blame, but studies also revealed that when institutions match younger women with high-ranking female academics to try to counter this, it had the opposite effect. Those high-ranking academics made the younger women feel like impostors, who would always fall short in comparison to such superwomen.

The irony here is that those superwomen probably experienced plenty of their own impostorism, but because we can only ever compare our own inner world with other people's outer world, we never get the inside track on their insecurities. The reality is, only absolute idiots never feel like an impostor or a fraud, but because Impostor Syndrome is insidious and generates such introversion ('I'm not meant to be here, but the worst thing would be if anyone found out. Therefore the most important thing is to keep my head down and hope no one does' no one ever talks about it. So our 'superwoman' boss or colleague, who appears super-competent, organised and collected may be making us feel like a fraud, but she's probably battling all of the same thoughts and feelings (irony of ironies, maybe about you) and doesn't feel she can talk about it.

I can see why this is: the idea of the career superwoman is still so prized that when she appears before us ticking all those boxes (efficient, decisive, composed, stylish, swishy hair), she takes on a deity-like status – something 'other' that we mere mortals could never live up to. Until you find out she's no more of a deity than Beyoncé, and thinks the same about you.

Perspective helps a little – some of the women I thought were the very epitome of unattainable collected profession-alism at the start of my career have since shared stories of the chaos that surrounded their personal and professional lives in their twenties and thirties. Stories that I never would have guessed at when I was starting out – they were my scary boss-ladies, who never made mistakes. Until they did.

I'm pretty sure that to some of the women (and men) who worked for my mum, she was the scary boss-lady. Apart from everything I've heard anecdotally (including several of her former colleagues and employees saying she was 'amazing but intimidating'), I can imagine how her prodigious work ethic and insane levels of organisation would have made me feel as a young woman working for her. Like a massive impostor.

But, in reality, no one I've spoken to has been able to describe having Impostor Syndrome as well as my mum could because, over the course of her forty-year career, she had it in spades.

'Throughout my career, I often had the sense of being an impostor, who was not good enough for the job, and that one day I would be "found out",' she told me. 'At one point in my career, I was working as head of investor relations for a major utility company and this lack of belief in my credentials for the role led me to undertake a master's degree in finance, to better equip me for the job.'

And does she believe it's a uniquely female trait?

She's not so sure. 'I've always worked in male-dominated sectors, but the women I've worked alongside – particularly those in senior roles – seemed comfortable in their roles, with good self-esteem. If anything, I felt like the exception. I think class can play a role. I suspect that Impostor Syndrome doesn't affect too many privately educated middle-class men or women, in whom a particular sense of entitlement and self-confidence has been instilled from an early age.'

I suspect she's right. But also my mum's assessment that most of her colleagues seemed comfortable in their roles highlights just how insidious Impostor Syndrome is: how could she have known? After all, I'm sure my mother will have projected an air of total confidence to her colleagues, so who knows how many of them also secretly felt they were winging it?

As I've already said, the only people who never feel impostorism are probably total idiots and, to an extent, I can see how a modicum of it could be a good thing. It's certainly kept me on my toes and stopped me getting complacent about my job. But it's also held me back because it's encouraged me to spend more time comparing myself to other people than focusing on the task at hand.

There's nothing like a good dose of Impostor Syndrome to stifle productivity and creativity. Time spent in a meeting sulkily contemplating how Susan from Marketing had that really great idea that you really should have come up with isn't time well spent. It's also held me back in all the projects or jobs I haven't gone for. All the times I haven't put myself forward for a promotion and all the times I've procrastinated so long about deciding on a job that I've taken myself out of the running. To some people, feeling out of your depth is a challenge to be grasped with both hands. To me, it's the worst feeling in the world and something to be avoided.

The link between my Impostor Syndrome and my Beta-ness is complex. On one hand, many of the Alpha women I spoke to talked about feeling like a fraud if they didn't meet the impossibly high standards they'd set themselves – the fact that they were Alpha didn't stop them having Impostor Syndrome. It fuelled it.

But if Impostor Syndrome has held me back, how much has being a Beta done so? What if I'm worse at my job in some ways because of certain aspects of my personality?

I've talked about the positive traits of being a Beta boss, but what about the toxic elements of Beta-ness? Does my laid-back attitude equal sloppiness? I don't enjoy confrontation, but does this mean I don't push my team enough to do the best job they can, or that I don't stand up for myself enough? I've certainly been told that I need to be 'more of a diva' to fight for what my team and I need from other departments, and I'm sure that's just one of many ways that my turning on more Alpha would make me better at my job.

Just as not all bosses have to be Alpha, Beta doesn't automatically mean better. It's about balance, and I can't say I always get there.

For example, I very much believe that a role will shrink or expand to fit the person inhabiting it. Injecting a certain amount of ego into your interactions, pushing boundaries and taking on more work, you can make your role and yourself far more significant than someone who does the job asked of them but doesn't look beyond it. This is especially so when you work in an industry with ill-defined job titles or boundaries.

I sometimes wonder if the role I'm in becomes smaller for having me in it. An element of that is probably because my ego doesn't get too involved. Maybe you need ego, drive and single-minded determination to move things along. That doesn't mean we all have to be like that all of the time, but surely if embracing a more Alpha outlook from time to time will help me see a project through to its final conclusion, or deal with a difficult team member, then I should do it. As for shouting louder, getting noticed, making things all about me, it might make me cringe, I might be at odds with my very Beta sensibility that you shouldn't make a fuss or shout about your achievements or take credit for anything you ever do . . . but it's just good PR, isn't it?

We can get bogged down with all the things that may be wrong with an Alpha boss. The dogmatism, the temper tantrums, the penchant for self-promotion above all else can be a nightmare when you're working for a nightmare. But the right Alpha, who is emotionally intelligent and mindful, can be a spectacular and inspiring boss. In fact, as a Beta who is incredibly comfortable with being told what to do, I've loved working for Alpha women because I've always felt they inspire and drive people in a way that I may not always manage.

Eddie Erlandson agrees that it's important to get out of the mindset that an Alpha boss is automatically a 'bad boss'. 'These are people who get things done, they have many, many, many strengths and they have a few "underbellies", as we say – a few weaknesses.' And, crucially, Alphas have a dynamism that, if channelled in the right way, can be really powerful. 'One thing I love about Alphas is, if they want to change, they can do it overnight,' Erlandson goes on. 'They can be stubborn and they can be difficult to work with, but when they decide they're going to shift something, either in themselves or in their behaviour, they do it, whether they're male or female. That's what I love about working with them.'

Maybe it is a fundamental personality trait – I always feel that being constantly Alpha would involve a huge reserve of energy that I don't have. And maybe if it feels exhausting and like an act I shouldn't be doing it. But what if that's a cop-out? What if my Impostor Syndrome is actually the impostor here?

And rather than dressing it up as a cute or endearing character trait, or a blueprint for great future leaders, is it possible that Beta-ness (specifically my Beta-ness) comes from laziness? What if my desire to be liked is greater than my desire to do my job to the best of my abilities? What if I'm opting out just because I can?

I don't *think* I am, but it's something worth considering

– not least because the amount of privilege attached to my potential professional laziness is huge.

Maybe being 'not Alpha' is a choice – it's me opting out of the hard stuff other people have to do every day at work. The difficult decisions, difficult conversations, working ultra-hard and risking being disliked because it's the right thing to do. Maybe I prize too much being liked above being right.

And that applies to all life, not just work. 'But don't you ever just want to stay in bed?' I asked Jemma, who used to work for me, when we were talking about her seemingly endless energy, her desire to do and see everything.

Her answer cut short my certainty that a four-hour lie-in is the best place to be on a Saturday morning. 'We're in such a place of privilege and I have so much life for the taking that why would I not go and take it?' she asked. 'So, I could stay in bed until eleven a.m., or I could get up at seven and go to some incredible spinning class and an amazing brunch with interesting people.

'I love bed, but I feel that bed is an opportunity that everyone has, whereas I have the privilege that I have access to these other things, which I feel very lucky that I do, so I try to take them by the balls.'

By opting out of stuff, am I exercising my right to be who I want to be in the workplace, or am I too lazy to make the most of opportunities that I'm lucky enough to have?

There's no way of dressing it up: I'm a white, cis-gender, university-educated, middle-class woman, who works in a female-dominated industry. I've got privilege coming out of my ears. I work hard, yes, but lots of people work hard.

I'm good at my job, but so are lots of people. But also I've been lucky, and I exist in a structure that naturally works in favour of people like me. And I love my job, but do I love it enough? Do I approach it with enough gusto? Is 'good enough' adequate when I know, in my heart of hearts, that talent and hard work has only got me so far?

Maybe I'd be more of an Alpha if I'd had a harder time starting out. If I'd had to graft a bit more at the beginning, elbow a few more people out of the way, I might have developed a few more edges. Or I might have given up completely, and moved into a less competitive profession. Maybe the reason so many female editors are Alphas, or at least appear to be, is because if you don't learn how to assert yourself, and how to shout the loudest, you don't get very far. What if I'm the anomaly because I got lucky?

Or, as I said earlier, perhaps the reason I've done okay, and survived in a fairly turbulent industry, is because of my innate Beta-ness, not in spite of it. I took on work that other people might have turned up their noses at because I've never been particularly snobby or ego-driven about the type of work I do. Or, to be fair, very focused on my career path. But, as it happened, it made my experience far more diverse and future-proofed my career in a way that evaded some of my colleagues. My pragmatism worked in my favour but that was through chance rather than design – which sounds like a very Beta path to success, if you ask me.

I suppose what it comes down to is how much my, or anyone else's, Beta-ness is a fundamental personality trait, and how much you can change it. If I demonstrated greater willpower, could I force myself to become an Alpha boss?

Would that make me better at my job or would I – would most people – eventually crack under the pressure?

And say I could fight it, say I got souped up on Berocca and started tackling each day like a true Alpha, would that make me better at work? At life? I suspect the answer would be sort of yes, sort of no. I'd get used to some aspects of it, I'm sure, but maybe the pressure of constantly being on would make me a total misery to be around. And, yes, I could start pushing my team harder, but in the process I would become totally unapproachable. It's a trade-off, and I'm not sure that anyone ever gets the balance right. And I believe balance is all we should be aiming for. I should always try my hardest, I should always push things, and push myself a little harder than I'm comfortable with – because otherwise what's the point? I should always remember how lucky I am to be in the position I'm in, and I should do everything I can to bring as many women up with me. But should I stop being true to myself and who I am? Should I lose all sense of authenticity? I suspect the answer is no.

And that's why we're here. We (women) feel like impostors because there are so few working environments, particularly in the corporate world, where we feel we automatically or instantly fit. We either change to fit in and feel like an impostor or we stay true to ourselves and feel like an outsider because we just don't fit. So where's the middle ground? I can't imagine a man having the same internal dialogue about staying true to himself versus fitting into a working environment, but maybe I'm wrong.

So when – and how – will it change? If Impostor Syndrome is a symptom of so many of us working in environments where we feel we don't fit, do we need to stop trying? Is it time we stopped trying to squeeze into the spaces we're given, and let the spaces expand or contract to fit us instead?

'Authenticity' is a buzzword, but it's vital if we want to retain our sense of self in a world that rewards homogeneity. Alpha or Beta, the only way we'll stop feeling like impostors is if we start being honest about who we are and what we bring to the table, rather than trying to fit into a one-size-fits-all template of a working woman. Easier said than done? Of course. But if we took all the energy we put into questioning ourselves and used it elsewhere, think what we could achieve.

6.

I think, if pressed (or if I had to find a good way of opening a chapter), I'd call myself a girl's girl, or a woman's woman, depending on where you fall on that particular debate. Not because I don't have any male friends, or because I particularly enjoy walking down the street arm in arm with my three besties while the Sugababes blasts out from a giant speaker in the sky, but because I like other women, I 'get' most women and, with a few exceptions, I can normally find a way to get on with them when I meet them. I certainly don't subscribe to the belief that women are 'too bitchy' or 'two-faced' or 'not as straightforward as men'. Obviously some women are some of these things but so are some men. I've never found female friendship difficult to negotiate, or that working primarily for or with other women for the majority of my career has ever been an issue. Quite the opposite. I thrive in all-female environments.

This is partly because I've worked mostly with brilliant, original, passionate, smart women, and have found it a pleasure to collaborate with them on a project. But it's not just about the work we do: the atmosphere a female team engenders (in my experience) can be supportive, fun, empathetic and nurturing. And, if I'm honest, I also love those little things that happen in a team of women who truly feel they're able to be themselves in the office. Like when

97

the makeup-remover wipes that someone bought when she was going to the gym at lunchtime magically spawn toothpaste, a tinted moisturiser, a pair of straighteners and some mascara that turn into a communal emergency going out/ walk of shame kit without anyone saying anything (and everyone on the team takes turns to replace things quietly when they run out). Or when new team members shyly become friends at the work Christmas party, or Friday-night drinks, then start hanging out together at weekends or become flatmates. Female office relationships can be fraught and tricky, but they can also be essential to surviving life at work.

My innate Beta-ness definitely helps here: my instinct is to fit in with other people, not to make a fuss and go where I'm needed. With every new job I've ever had, my desire to find a common ground with the team and just get on with it has overridden any shyness.

But it's more complicated now that I'm a boss. It becomes far more obvious how Beta I am when you see me interact with Alpha women. I have plenty of traits that could be considered Alpha, and there are plenty of scenarios throughout the working day to back that up – when I'm running our morning news conference and deciding which stories we're going to cover that day, or making a call on how we spend our budget. I know they're part of my job, I know how to deal with them, and I can do them well because I've done these things before. But put me in a room with a group of Alpha women and it quickly becomes obvious just how Beta I am. I can't compete and I simply don't want to.

My natural role is conflict negotiator. When I'm in a

room full of Alpha women, I am more about managing their egos and respective agendas than pushing my own. The downside of this is obvious – I don't always get to push my own agenda, and this is to my detriment. But the upside is that people generally like working and dealing with me – they know I won't be a pain in the bottom and that, generally, stuff will get done. This means that, in turn, they're more likely to do me a favour when I ask for it. So, sometimes my agenda still gets pushed, just in a more roundabout way.

The first time I realised there was power to be had in being, essentially, the pushover of the team (as I was seen at the time) occurred when I was still very junior, an editorial assistant, and I found myself dealing with a particularly tricky client who had fallen out with my (Alpha) boss and my boss's boss. But she'd still deal with me. From her point of view this was because she believed I was so junior that she'd get her own way. But the more I dealt with her, occasionally cajoling her into doing things our way, working out which stuff we could push back on and which we could use as a bargaining chip on other matters, I realised she was basically happy to defer to our judgement on any number of things. There were a few issues she wouldn't move on, but otherwise she just wanted to be asked. She wanted to feel that the end result was down to her work, her ideas and her judgement as much as ours.

It took me ages, but eventually we got a final product signed off that everyone was happy with. You could argue that I got there by being a creep, but I like to think I did it by being nice (and protecting my client's ego by putting mine to one side). It earned me a small promotion (and the dubious honour of dealing with the aforementioned tricky client going forward).

You'll notice that I've only talked about Alpha women here. And that's because I've found that I operate differently when I'm dealing with Alpha men. I don't know the rules as well, I don't get them, and I'm not sure where I exist in the hierarchy (if at all). It's probably because I've almost always worked with other women, but when I have to operate in an environment with primarily brash Alpha men, I find myself disengaging completely. Would I operate differently among men if I were more Alpha? Almost certainly.

I suppose the part of this that intrigues me most is how we treat female relationships in the workplace: I feel I instinctively know the rules when I'm dealing with most women, but I couldn't tell you where I learnt them. Popular culture has about as much to say on female working relationships as it does on how women behave in the workplace (not much, applied with broad brushstrokes). With a few notable exceptions (*Working Girl*, *The Devil Wears Prada*), they don't get a look-in at all. And when they do, two women are generally pitted against each other, one good, one evil (and, more often than not, the good Beta versus the evil Alpha). But there's certainly no room for nuance, or real life.

It's another symptom of the wider issue we discussed earlier: the narrow way in which women are depicted in popular culture, and how that impacts on our IRL expectations of women at work. 'It's almost as though if you are a powerful woman in a Hollywood film you basically are going to be either the evil Maleficent or you're going to be presented as very unhappy. So you're either really nasty or really unhappy or you're both,' agrees Caroline Hedleman, research director for the Geena Davies Institute.

And when we do study all-female teams, or female working relationships, the focus is on the supposed negatives – none of which has anything to do with work or a workplace. Here's a sample from a first-person interview given to the *Daily Mail* in 2009 by Samantha Brick. 'I was often out trying to win contracts, but back at the office, work was an afterthought. It came second to conversations about shopping, boyfriends and diets – oh, and spiteful comments from my two research assistants who were sharpening their claws against another staff member, Natasha.'

Brick then goes on to describe how one of said research assistants went on to terrorise poor Natasha, while the (also female) general manager refused to step in for fear of being the 'bad cop'. Brick also mentions that the atmosphere improved measurably every time a couple of freelance men were introduced into the office, and that, overall, the team became more productive with that crucial injection of testosterone into the mix. (She supposes this was because her employees 'were too busy flirting'.)

Obviously I have no idea what went on in that company, but Brick's implication – that the women's sex lives, love of fashion and diets ruled the office, and they behaved like that only because there were no men around to temper their behaviour – is bizarre, reductive and unhelpful (and, obviously, what Brick was doing to manage this team is never mentioned). But the most troubling part of the article is that those women, and this torrid, barely believable tale, are obviously meant to be a proxy for all women in the workplace. It feeds into a dangerous wider narrative that women can only exist at work in the context of men. Without that all-important injection of testosterone, an office becomes a coven.

And this ties into a wider point as to why there's so little conversation in the media, in popular culture, about female-dominated teams or offices: we simply don't see women collectively as protagonists in an office environment. There may be a boss-lady, but if she were in a film, she'd be a plot point all on her own. Individuals learning how to thrive in a male-dominated environment is one thing, but women existing as a professional team with its own internal hierarchies and politics, getting a job done with no male input? Nah. No one will watch that.

There's also a mistaken and rarely questioned assumption that the only women inhabiting senior roles in most workplaces will be quite Alpha. I say 'mistaken assumption' because I think that, whatever her personality type, for a woman to thrive in an almost entirely male environment, she would feel the need to adopt as Alpha a persona as she could.

Look at it this way. According to the FTSE Woman Leaders Review 2016, twelve FTSE 100 companies still have all-male executive committees, and while the number of women on boards for FTSE companies is on the rise, the numbers are still woefully low – ranging from 21.1 per cent to 26.6 per cent – and almost all non-executive directors are men. The glass ceiling is still very much a reality, and it creates an environment in which women are allowed to behave in only one way – as close to adopting as masculine a persona as possible.

But there is huge value in understanding inter-female

relationships in the workplace, not least because women interact and operate with each other differently from men, and sometimes with levels of nuance and subtlety that can't be found in male relationships.

'Working on an all-female team has been a dream – this sounds like hyperbole but it's true,' says Danielle, twenty-eight. 'Everyone is supportive of one another and problems are discussed, which means they are resolved quickly. On a mostly male team I felt frustrated often and as though my voice was stifled. There was a combative and competitive atmosphere, which, in the end, exhausted me.'

Naomi, the thirty-three-year-old project manager I mentioned earlier, also feels it was easier to get stuff done on an all-female team. 'In the construction industry for six years, I have worked with mainly male teams for the entirety of this time. It's an aggressive atmosphere – competitive and process-driven rather than with any personal goals or connections. I had previously worked in an all-female team in aviation and found it to be a much more supportive and encouraging environment.'

There have been lots of studies into the relative productivity and harmony of all-male or all-female teams versus mixed-gender groups. A study by the Massachusetts Institute of Technology (MIT) and George Washington University published in 2014 found, for example, that employee morale and satisfaction were higher on single-sex teams, but groups that had a more diverse gender spread were more productive and produced higher revenues. The reason for the higher satisfaction levels in single-gender teams is simple – and explains why I find female colleagues easier to deal with than men. In the words of the study's co-author, Sara Fisher Ellison, speaking to the *Wall Street Journal*, 'People are more comfortable around people who are like them.' She also speculated that single-sex teams 'socialise more and work less', hence the dip in productivity.

In another study – also by George Washington University – more than three hundred management students were randomly assigned teams, some predominately male or female and others gender-balanced. The study found that men in teams with a balanced gender mix had a more positive experience than those in teams dominated by men. The study also found that the mixed-gender teams tended to out-perform the predominately single-sex teams.

'We examined the impact of team gender on several variables important to team success, including trust, cohesion, inclusion and task/relationship conflict,' said Kaitlin Thomas, a doctoral candidate in industrial-organisational psychology at George Washington. One reason for this, she suggests, is that women tend to be more relationship-oriented than men so place more focus on collaboration within the team.

Whatever the gender mix of the offices I've been in, one thing has consistently got me through the day when things have been hard: my work friendships. And although these are often the women we see more than anyone else, those work friendships aren't explored or celebrated enough. They can be crucially important when it comes to looking at how women progress in a workplace that is still in many ways pitched against them.

We haven't worked together for almost a decade, but Christina was my first – and best – work wife. She picked me up when I fell backwards off the stage at the office Christmas party, and let me crash on her sofa the following year when I lost all my possessions and couldn't get into my flat. We've travelled from Caracas to Kiev together and still go on holiday when we can, children and partners allowing. When she got married I was her bridesmaid.

But the defining moment when I realised she was my work wife happened eight years ago when I was made redundant from the company we worked at together. It was my first job, and I'd been there almost four years. I kind of knew it was time to leave, and it wasn't the biggest shock in the world but, still, no one *really* expects that conversation on a Monday afternoon. I wouldn't have bought all my lunches for the week from the supermarket next door an hour earlier if I had.

After being told I was probably losing my job, I went straight to the pub and called Christina, who came straight away with my handbag, which I'd left behind. She stayed all evening, and took me for dinner in an attempt to sober me up, offering me a space in her bed if I didn't want to go home on my own. She said she'd clear my desk for me, too, so I wouldn't have to go back to the office if I didn't want to.

And that's why a work wife is brilliant: she's somewhere between your colleague, who totally gets why you hate Claire, the office manager, with a passion, and your best friend, who gets you, but rolled into one person.

Having a 'work wife' is good for your career. According to a 2016 study by the guys at CV-library, 47.2 per cent of UK professionals either have or wish they had a 'work spouse'. Respondents cited the benefits as 'offering support and mentorship, providing advice and guidance and offering friendship and companionship'.

Another study shows that 50 per cent of those with a best friend at work feel they have a strong connection with the company, and 70 per cent of employees say having friends at work is the most crucial part of a happy working life.

I keep referring to a 'work wife' – because who doesn't love alliteration? – and we are looking at female friendships, but I am, of course, referring to a work spouse. They are your work 'person', someone who has your back in any situation, will give you proper good advice, and will never stab you in the back just to get in there with Geoff from Procurement.

She (or he) is the person you make a pact with before the Christmas party to whisk you away when you start to get 'boozy melted face', which means you're about to do something bad, because you know she'll be keeping an eye out and will move heaven and earth to ensure you don't get caught feeling up that new guy from Finance in the disabled toilets. She's the person you can complain to about your boss without fear of reprisals. She's also the person who will give you proper objective career advice when you're not sure what your next move should be, if you messed up that presentation, or whether you should be going for that promotion. It also means you've always got someone to go to lunch with.

A good work wife is – or should be – the absolute opposite of Samantha Brick's deranged depiction of an all-female working environment. It should be the epitome, the absolute pinnacle, of female colleague-dom. It's not the same as a mentor, or a boss who really cares about your personal development, or even that fun colleague with great gossip about the team on the third floor. It's someone who understands you and the job you do better than anyone else in the world. They know why you care because they care too. They aren't going to roll their eyes when you mention for the fourteenth time how annoying you find Claire because they 100 per cent feel your pain. And they can also tell you, better than anyone else in the world, when it's time for you to go. If your work wife tells you you're wasted where you are, or that it's time to move on, that's excellent advice, worth taking into serious consideration. Because no one cuts their work wife loose – and potentially loses the only person in the office up for a hung-over Nando's at lunchtime – unless they really mean it.

'I think, when you're in a very male environment, a lot of it is about having that constant ally,' explains Sara, who works in the science department of a university. 'My best friend and I worked together for four years, and having that person who totally had my back was amazing. It meant I was able to relax into the job more than I probably do now we're not working together.'

But, as with all human interactions, it's complicated, as Sara explains: 'I tend to gravitate towards other women when we work together, but some women are really anti that and push you away a bit – I think they see it as a sign of weakness. But everyone's different, I guess.'

For Cara, forty, who has worked in marketing in London and Canada (so has had to find her feet in new office environments and a new country), work wives have punctuated some of the most important moments of her career.

'Over the years I've had several work wives (and even a work husband!) and I can honestly say these women have helped me get through some of the most challenging moments of my career. It's just so nice to have someone "human" to connect with at work and look forward to seeing every day. The ability to sneak away for a quick chat and ask for helpful advice from someone you trust is a huge perk of having a work wife. You never have to worry about eating lunch alone, and she is always up for a cheeky coffee run to Starbucks or a little nip outside to get air.'

And, as Cara learnt, a good work wife should enhance the rest of your life: 'I recently celebrated a milestone birthday and had an afternoon-tea party with a number of friends who didn't know each other. As the ladies chatted and established how they knew me, it quickly became apparent that 90 per cent of the guests were women I had worked with over the years. That bit was amazing – my work wives were meeting each other and sharing funny stories about our escapades together. It really made me realise how blessed I've been to have worked with such awesome females and I'm so glad that I've maintained the relationships even after moving on to different roles.'

I totally agree. When I was organising my hen do, I wanted it to be fairly small, so I invited only the women I'm closest to. Two-thirds of the guest list was comprised of women I had worked with in some capacity over the last decade.

In a 2016 study by the University of Pennsylvania and Arizona State University of the relationships between female baboons (stick with me here), they discovered that, although the males leave the group once they've grown up and go to join another group (where they have to fight their way to the top hierarchy), females stay with the same group from birth. They inherit their position within it (Alpha, Beta, Gamma and so on) from their mothers. Scientists also discovered that these hierarchies remained stable with almost no change for fifteen, twenty or thirty years.

It was assumed that evolution dictates that those baboons with the most Alpha-like traits are most likely to survive and pass them on to their daughters. In fact, it turns out that the baboons that did best were those that had the strongest relationships with other females in the group – the same females, year after year. This was so for groups thousands of miles apart, and feels strangely reminiscent of numerous studies that have found our relationships with other people are the key to our happiness.

In the case of the baboons, scientists found that those who were the most closely bonded with other females in their group had the lowest levels of stress hormones. This makes sense: they supported each other in disputes, their friendship generated fewer disputes over food, and they'd groom each other a lot, which everyone knows is the best stress-buster there is. They're each other's work wives, and they're happier, less stressed, and thrive as a result.

With good reason, I've banged on at length about the virtues of working with women and having fantastic female working relationships. It's my friendships at work that have made terrible jobs bearable, and great jobs out-of-this-world amazing. I've worked with women far more than I have with men, so it's those relationships that stand out for me. I stay in touch with most of my old female work friends far more than I do with male former colleagues. This means plenty of opportunity to rehash funny or scandalous work stories. Our friendships and our time at work together develop a mythical status with each retelling to a new boyfriend or friend-of-a-friend who joins the group. Even the most dull, banal or depressing jobs take on a rosy glow when revisited with my work wives.

But what if female friendships don't work for you? Or if they do, but you don't like, or get, your female colleagues? Not every all-female team is a pulsating mass of oestrogen ready to explode at any moment, but neither is every experience of an all-female working environment going to be positive.

Take Natalie, thirty-four, whose experience of an all-female PR team in her early twenties made her avoid them thereafter: 'The senior managers, who were all at least a decade older than us juniors, bitched about us in private and openly. It was different if you were one of their chosen ones whom they'd support blindly – the office was incredibly cliquey – but if they took against you that was it.'

And, of course, sometimes it's a mixed bag – just like working in an all-male team. 'It has been both,' says Sue, a fifty-seven-year-old management trainer. 'The male environment was straightforward, hard-working, focused on achieving goals, but lacked heart and the desire to do the right thing by people. The female environment felt more complicated – lots of decision-makers, creative, a bit catty, but good fun and value-based.'

Obviously it depends on the job, on the team, on the boss and the mix of people. Gender is an element, but it's one of many. For me, it almost always works and I see working in a female-dominated environment as a privilege.

But either way you cut it, it's clear – and shouldn't even need noting – that how women deal with each other at work is just as complex and deserves just as much airtime as how we deal with men, how they deal with us, and how men in the workplace interact with each other. Yet unless it's to highlight some extremely unpleasant behaviour or to muse on how pregnancy affects a woman's ability to behave rationally in a professional setting, the inner workings and dynamics of a female team are rarely considered in popular culture or the media.

How we are perceived as individual women in the workplace is the thin end of the wedge – it's indicative of the wider picture around how women are viewed in the workplace. And equally, how we are perceived as a group, or how women are perceived within a team, is crucially important. The collective noun for a group of female colleagues working together towards a common goal should be 'team', not 'coven' – the actual term used to describe one of my all-female teams. By a bloke, of course. You can be as Alpha or as Beta as you like, but if you're not allowed to exist in relation to other women in a professional sense in the workplace, that all becomes pretty academic.

When someone says, writes or indeed tweets something stupid, offensive or in some cases downright dangerous, the race to call them out for it on social media is a reflection of what goes on in meeting rooms around the country every day but on a more terrifying scale. There's a certain weird kudos in being the one who spotted it first. In having that thing to say that everyone is agreeing with. Opinion – especially negative opinion – is currency and everyone wants to record the best opinion first.

The mundane IRL version of that? A regional sales meeting in which someone gives a perfectly adequate presentation that one of his bosses criticises as 'just not what I had in mind' and . . . leaving it at that. Which is basically shorthand for 'I dislike your ideas for non-specific reasons, but I want to get my bit in before anyone else and I haven't had time to form a proper opinion.'

Because Boss Number One has said something, the race is on for everyone else to get in with their feedback before someone else says it first. Everyone's attempting to make that one, incisive, cutting observation that nails what the problem is with Gareth's (let's call him Gareth) presentation. In the end, Boss Number Six, panicked at having said nothing so far, pointedly remarks that Gareth neglected to use the company colours on slide seventeen. Everyone else nods thoughtfully. The next day Gareth is signed off work with stress.

How do you show the world how Alpha you are? You talk a lot and slag everyone else off. It's a ruse as old as time (probably) and, often, it works. Most people are busy dealing with their own stuff, so they tend to assume that if someone is vocal, self-assured and sounds knowledgeable (read: has a loud voice), they must know what they're talking about.

And the best way to really nail your Alpha-ness? By saying, repeatedly, how useless everyone else is. Of course, a true Alpha, who was confident of his or her place in the Alpha food chain, would never bother with that sort of rubbish. They're too busy building empires to keep talking about the time Mhairi in Accounts messed up the projections for Q4. But an insecure person trying to assert themselves as head honcho? They're slagging off Mhairi's rudimentary grasp of Excel to everyone who will listen.

Whether you're Alpha or Beta, being on the receiving end of spurious criticism happens to us all. And neither Alphas nor Betas will do it more: it's about competence, not personality types. If you're good at your job you won't need to. But the difference is in how we respond – and that's why we're talking about it here. While an Alpha woman may instantly question or confront criticism, a Beta woman may internalise it – and start to believe it (as I certainly have done). But understanding what motivates others, and learning how to negotiate tricky and toxic working environments without compromising our sense of self, is vital for any Beta in the workplace.

My friend Alice works in the civil service, and recalls

dealing with a notoriously incompetent senior manager, who has the added delightful reputation for being really difficult. 'She's rude, aggressive and dismissive,' Alice explains, after yet another run-in with said manager. (Incidentally, Alice is very good at her job. You know how with some people you just know?) 'Her first response to any question or proposal is always "No." I've seen her make some truly terrible judgement calls as a result. She obviously knows she's got a rubbish reputation and this is her way of reminding everyone that she's the boss. In reality people are just less forgiving when she messes up, because no one likes her.'

Alice doesn't necessarily think she is the worst manager she deals with – but she's the one who sticks in her mind because this woman has invested so much time in making life difficult for everyone else.

I ask Alice if she thinks her boss would get away with that sort of behaviour if she were a man. 'Probably,' she concedes. 'If she was a man people would still note how incompetent she is, but I don't think her overall attitude would have been mentioned in the same way because the expectation would have been different. If a male manager is rude, that's just the way it is. If a woman is rude, it's a conversation topic for everyone else.'

In Alice's boss, her rudeness, her refusal to agree to anything may be a defence mechanism born of insecurity and what sounds like incompetence. And I understand how being critical or negative can be seen as shorthand for being good at your job. After all, according to Conservative MP Kenneth Clarke, Theresa May is a 'bloody difficult woman', the implication being that, like her predecessor Margaret

Thatcher, she is competent (although 'difficult' is an interesting choice of word, did he mean that she may be competent but she's still a pain because she's making life harder for men like Clarke)?

But saying no all the time means you have a critical mind, you're an analytical genius who can get straight to the heart of the problem. It never occurs to anyone that saying no all the time could be as much a sign of indecisiveness as it is in the person who says, 'I don't know' sixteen times a day. At the other end of the spectrum is the person who says 'Yes' all the time. She's a pushover: who would want to be her?

So saying 'no', always finding fault, jumping in with your criticism before anyone else does is a defensive move, designed to shine a light on other people's shortcomings and blind people to your own.

But the inner politics of the AGM at a plastic-bottle manufacturer in the Home Counties is one thing. What about when criticism one-upmanship takes place on a macro level? What happens when you're Twitter-shamed?

You may be familiar with the story of Justine Sacco. In 2013, she was senior director of Corporate Communications for IAC, an American media and internet company. She made the news when she travelled from New York to South Africa to visit family, tweeting during a stopover: *Going to Africa. Hope I don't get AIDs. Just kidding. I'm white!*

She switched her phone off, spent the next eleven hours on a plane to Cape Town and landed to discover that her tweet had been retweeted three thousand times and she had been fired. Not only were people outraged, the public shaming of Sacco quickly became a form of fun – as Jon

Ronson notes when he interviews her in his book *So You've Been Publicly Shamed*:

> The furor over Sacco's tweet had become not just an ideological crusade against her perceived bigotry, but also a form of idle entertainment. Her complete ignorance of her predicament for those eleven hours lent the episode both dramatic irony and a pleasing narrative arc. As Sacco's flight traversed the length of Africa, a hashtag started to trend worldwide #HasJustineLandedYet.

One Twitter user went to the airport to tweet her arrival, taking her photo and posting it on the internet.

In the same book, Ronson has talked about the pleasure and satisfaction he has taken in the past from joining in with the public shaming of someone who has said or done something deemed offensive or distasteful. 'In the early days of Twitter I was a keen shamer. When newspaper columnists made racist or homophobic statements, I joined the pile-on. Sometimes I led it.'

He recalls the satisfaction he took from being one of the first people to alert social media to the story the late A. A. Gill wrote about shooting a baboon on safari, partly because 'Gill always gave my television documentaries bad reviews, so I always keep a vigilant eye on things he could be got for.' Ronson's tweet did the trick: 'Within minutes it was everywhere. Amid the hundreds of congratulatory messages, one stuck out: "Were you a bully at school?"'

Where did the satisfaction come from? Was it in spotting it first? In being the person who made it go viral? Or is the value, when you're highlighting someone's offensiveness on social media, in being able to dish out the most incisive criticism? The most acerbic? In being the one person who can best explain What Is Wrong With the World in 140 characters?

When Polly Vernon released her book *Hot Feminist* in 2015, she expected it to cause controversy. The reviews were mixed – and a couple were particularly damning. She wasn't expecting the subsequent barrage of abuse she received from hundreds of women who were, in her words, 'all keen to tell me how stupid my book and I were'. She later wrote about the experience in the *Guardian*: 'I'd been destabilised by Twitter's rush to shame me. Shame: such a distinct, old-fashioned – old – feeling. Exactly the sort of thing you might feel, if hundreds of disembodied voices turned on you, denounced you, shunned you.'

Now Polly tells me, 'I think that we are operating in a time when it does inform reviews and critics in that if you want to cause a big old fuss and get retweeted hugely then to really take issue with something is one easy way to do that. A really brilliant woman told me that she was approached by someone for a negative quote for my book, and she said, "I haven't read it," and they said, "That doesn't matter."' She adds, 'It would have been horrible but I would have dealt with it, if it hadn't provoked this onslaught on Twitter – if I hadn't been the subject of this lampooning. It was a whole thing to prove you're a good feminist. It was not only okay to slag me off as a woman and a feminist, it made you look like a better feminist.'

Criticism had become currency: bad reviews drove traffic and online chat, and that online chat became a game of one-upmanship, with each user looking to out-damn the previous one.

And it happens every single day. Why do we do it?

Dr Bernie Hogan, of the Oxford Internet Institute, believes that social media simply mimic our real-life behaviour in this respect: 'There are a lot of cases where mob rule is the rule of the day – crowds and mobs have been a feature of human society for a very long time.

'Boundaries are really important for one's identity – and not just about being able to say, "I'm part of this group." It's about policing boundaries and saying who's in and who's out.'

Essentially, in a world where we're constantly looking for belonging or acceptance, we demonstrate who we're with and what we stand for in as broad a brushstroke as possible. But does Twitter make this worse?

'It doesn't necessarily amplify this process,' explains Dr Hogan, 'but it might make this process more likely because of the real lack of cues on Twitter. It's really hard to know which side someone is on. Furthermore, having a "side" will probably get you more retweets.'

Ah, yes, because opinion is currency.

People's desire to be on the 'right side' but also first can be seen when Ronson talks about Justine Sacco's story: 'I think self-righteous people who piled onto Justine Sacco, robbing her joke of its nuance and just trying to destroy her because they wanted to be seen as a kind of Rosa Parks – but of course they weren't, because there was nothing brave about it – they're more frightening, actually, than trolls.'

So, back to poor old Gareth and his mediocre presentation. He's not having to deal with hundreds of people telling him how lacklustre his PowerPoint game is, but he is the unwitting victim of six people vying for top-dog status, and there's no better way to prove you're right than to demonstrate that someone else is wrong.

And there's the classic not-wanting-to-admit-to-having-the-'wrong'-opinion – that is, one that's diametrically opposed to someone more senior – so you get in your criticism at the outset just to be on the safe side. I've definitely been guilty of this one. There have been points in my career where I've worked on hierarchical teams where (and this is crucial) I haven't been able to get to grips with what my editor wanted, what they did and didn't like from a writer, or why. Maybe it was my fault, maybe it was theirs but, for whatever reason, something was not clicking.

Part of my job was to take in copy from writers, give them initial feedback and make edits before passing to my boss. I later realised that I responded with some vague criticism to almost every piece I received – even when I was perfectly happy with it – getting the writer to make a few cursory (and probably pointless) amendments. I was essentially hedging my bets in case my editor didn't like the piece, in which case I could say, 'I don't like it either – I've already given them a load of amends, and it *still* isn't right.' If I'd had a better idea of what my boss was after, I'd have been able to give the writer a better brief in the first place, or gone back with the right sort of amendments. And if I'd had a bit more confidence I'd have stood up for a piece I loved and explained why I thought it was fine as it was, or asked the right sort of questions to get a better idea of what my editor actually wanted. But I didn't do either of those things. Instead I used criticism of someone else as a shield to disguise the fact that there were some bits of my job that I wasn't getting. I passed negative feedback uselessly up and down the food chain, without ever resolving what the problem was – because if it was someone else's fault, and someone else was being told they weren't getting it, no one was looking at me. And that, above all, was the main thing.

It was about me and it was about my boss. The only person it was never about was the writer.

It's hard to realise when you're in an office environment that has a steep, sometimes toxic hierarchy how much time people spend trying to shore up their own positions, rather than focusing on the task at hand. When you grasp that the vast majority of office interactions are nothing to do with you, it can feel incredibly freeing.

And it turns out we all remember that bad boss – the hyper-negative, overly critical one who made life a misery for everyone. And I have never heard a story like that where the team ended up being more productive as a result.

'I have experienced bosses who seemed to believe, mistakenly, that a negative managerial style would motivate their team to do better work,' explains Annie, who is a copywriter for a large retail brand, and has worked for retail or media brands throughout her career. 'Instead it just demoralised people, leaving them feeling that nothing they did could ever be good enough. In every instance it led to burnout and a culture of presenteeism. The best bosses lead by example and leave work on time and encourage their team to have a good work–life balance.'

Maybe I'm being a little hard on myself when I talk

about my own history of being overly and pointlessly critical. After all, I can remember that specific example so well because, for the most part, I hate giving people negative feedback and rarely do it. So when I do, I try hard to make the criticism as constructive as possible.

It's a rule I've stuck to fairly consistently ever since I got myself into that negative-feedback loop between my editor and the writers – I don't criticise people's work unless I can say what I don't like about it, or what I'd prefer instead. I see the dishing out of negative feedback as a tool that should be used sparingly and with care. It's my job to give my team feedback they can interpret properly to produce what I need. It's not their job to read my mind.

There's also a dangerous misconception that saying, 'I'm not sure,' or 'Can I just go away and think about it?' or keeping your mouth shut because you genuinely don't have a strong opinion on whatever's in front of you means you're indecisive and don't know what you want. Which is nonsense, because very few of the best decisions are made on a whim or a gut feeling, with little thought or consideration. 'Can I just go away and think about it?' should be the slogan of smart bosses everywhere, not a sign of weakness.

But it's not. Knowing what you want and what you think at all times are the hallmarks of a good boss. No one mentions what happens when the thing you want is the wrong thing and culminates in you sending your team down a rabbit hole of three months' pointless work. Thinking your opinions through before you share them never seems to be as valuable as just having an opinion.

We've all seen the statistic that men dominate 75 per

cent of the conversation on average in most meetings, and we all know, as we step into another meeting, whose voices we'll be hearing most for the next hour. They're not necessarily those of the smartest people in the room, but they're the loudest. And don't get me wrong: in a meeting full of women a couple of people will always emerge as the most outspoken in the same way. And when you don't have anything useful to say, what do you do? You complain about someone else.

But there's plenty of evidence to suggest that brevity is far more productive than talking just to fill the silence, as Joseph McCormack, author of *BRIEF: Making a Bigger Impact by Saying Less*, discovered. 'Brevity is an essential skill that can propel people's career in an age where the people that they're talking to are overwhelmed.' His point is that people tend to switch off after a certain point, and in many circumstances – a job interview, for example – rambling on makes you appear unprepared. He also believes we're conditioned to believe that when we over-explain something we demonstrate how smart we are – at school and university, essays are all about reaching the hallowed word count rather than what we have to say, and that attitude carries through into our adult lives.

But back to criticism. Obviously, not all criticism is created equal. Constructive criticism can be incredibly useful. (How individuals deal with constructive criticism is a whole other matter.) And critical thinking is vital in any business. My boss, for example, is far more likely to question what's in front of her than I am, and will robustly test the value of any new project or idea we have. But this stops me going off on a tangent every time I get enthused about an idea that doesn't necessarily have legs, or that I want to take up for no other reason than to keep someone else happy. My willingness to say yes can sometimes be a great thing, but you need someone else around to play a more questioning role.

Critical thinking isn't the same as toxic or hostile criticism, which can inhibit us from changing our behaviour or performance at work or school. Bad criticism is bad for everyone.

'You've got to start off by thinking about whether there's any truth in what this person is saying,' suggests Corinne Mills, a careers coach. 'Is it discomfiting because there's an element of truth or value in there? You have to consider whether this person is just being honest and start off with that position, but if you really feel like this isn't fair, and there's another agenda going on, then you'll know about it – you'll get a strong sense of being undermined.' And in those instances, Corinne says, it's rarely about you. 'Perhaps they don't realise they're doing it, there could be no agenda there at all. It could just be that they're not very soft-skilled. It's their style. There's no edge to it – they're just no good at dressing it up.'

But, of course, there may be another reason: 'Maybe they feel threatened by you, and keeping you down is a reflection of their insecurity and desire to keep you at bay. Or it could be transference, which is where you, for whatever reason, remind them of someone from their past or their family life – it could be an overbearing father or mother, an ex-husband – and they have a totally disproportionate reaction to you.'

'It's not you, it's me,' is never more true than when

looking at why you're getting unwarranted or constant criticism from your boss, or from a group of senior people in your organisation. For starters, the nine most common defence mechanisms, as defined by Anna Freud (her dad was a big deal) in her book *The Ego and the Mechanisms of Defence*, include displacement. Simply put, it's when someone is criticised by their boss or superior but is unable to display their anger or frustration with that person. Instead they take it out on an easier target: you. Basically, your boss has shifted their frustration away from the source of their anxiety to someone who will do them less harm.

And then there's the dynamic I mentioned above. The one where putting your head above the parapet and saying yes, or saying you like something, feels like a huge risk – and it's a risk your boss doesn't want to take. Maybe you work for a large organisation that's ruled by inertia and bureaucracy. Or maybe your boss's boss says 'No' all of the time, and that's the behaviour they've learnt. Or maybe they simply don't know what their superiors want from them so they're hedging their bets, as I did.

But what about when you work somewhere where saying 'No' and criticising other people is a power play? Not necessarily because it's intended to get someone else into trouble, but because, like Twitter, everyone is clamouring to get their really insightful piece of criticism in first to prove how invaluable they are to the process and the organisation? ('You couldn't possibly fire me, or not have me in this meeting,' they're trying to say. 'Look at all the costly embarrassing mistakes you'd end up making if I wasn't here to tell you all where you're going wrong!')

The irony is that constant negativity for the sake of it,

or criticising other people to shore up your own status, is something a true Alpha, who's confident in their position, would never do. They wouldn't have to.

Sir Richard Branson (the billionaire? Founder of the Virgin group? Yep, that guy) has said in the past that he was raised never to be nasty or negative about anyone, and claims it's a mantra he still lives by today. 'If I ever hear people gossiping about people I'll walk away. As a leader, you've just got to get out there and look for the best in people, and that's really, really important. Let them get on with it, not criticise them when they make mistakes, and praise them when they do good things.'

If you're someone who knows what you're doing and isn't afraid of being wrong, it costs a lot less to be nice. Certainly criticising people for the sake of it or as a reflex isn't the thing. But knowing when to give your team space to work things out for themselves, and letting them become okay with making mistakes and learning from them, is crucial.

As a freelancer I once did some work for a large retail brand and worked with two people in particular, a man and a woman. He was her boss, and it was pretty obvious he wasn't particularly good at his job. His instincts weren't great, and he seemed jealous of anyone who had the creative skills he clearly lacked. I think she was far more competent than he was – and when I had to deal with her directly, she was straightforward, positive and demonstrated decent instincts. But the minute he became involved in a meeting, the whole tone changed. My work – and other people's – would be criticised for reasons as broad and varied as 'I'm just not really feeling it' and 'This feels flat . . . I'm not sure why. Were you tired when you did this?'

Constructive criticism was not deemed necessary – in no small part because he didn't know how to give it. Which meant his weird, meaningless and always negative feedback became the benchmark against which everything was judged. And because he constantly used criticism of other people to shore up his own position ('If I know what you're doing wrong, when no one else can see it, then I must know what I'm doing'), his colleague started to do it too. I'd see her nervously glancing at him when they looked at a new piece of work, trying to gauge what he thought before stating her opinion (which was always negative).

I could even tell if he was standing next to her when she was on the phone to me, so different was the tone of the conversation. As far as he was concerned, she wasn't doing her job properly if she wasn't saying she hated something, so she complied. And she was stuck in that weird holding pattern where she had to keep him happy to avoid becoming the subject of his ire. It meant she couldn't do her job properly. What I've never been able to work out is the extent to which she thought he was right. Did she trust his instincts or just not trust her own? Did she believe his assertions that he was a creative genius and no one else was getting it, or did she know exactly what was going on, but was clinging grimly to her job for dear life? Probably a bit of everything.

When you create a situation where only negativity and criticism count, you end up existing in an environment where the only way people learn to assert themselves is by being critical and negative about others' work and behaviour. Social media can generate the same response, on a much larger scale, in which having an opinion first is the most important thing, and disagreeing with someone, or disputing their version of events, has far more currency than positive feedback. And not saying anything at all? Keeping your thoughts to yourself till you've really considered your response, or deciding that your opinion isn't needed in this instance? That's not an option. If you're not *seen* to be doing something, if you don't have an opinion, any opinion, you don't count. Because in a world where 140 characters can make you famous, it's what you say, not what you do, that counts.

It's hard to identify when you're on the receiving end of spurious criticism because it feels so personal: it's a direct attack on your work at best, or your character at worst. When I'm in a meeting where the tone is overly negative, and I can't work out if it's about the work at hand, or just the general vibe that's developed (on account of all the criticism one-upmanship), I like to imagine the whole thing is a race-to-the-finish computer game in which each player has to throw out as much criticism as they can before the timer goes so they can make it to the next round and face the evil boss. (See? It works on several levels.) Once you look at it in that way, you start to see how much it's about other people and not about you, which instantly makes it easier to deal with.

Another tactic? Criticise the criticism. If the feedback is unclear, or you're not sure what conclusions to draw from it, say so. If people are giving you conflicting criticism, or no way forward, say so. If the criticism directly contradicts what you were originally asked to do, and no one has acknowledged this, say so. Nothing will catch someone out in the act of lazy criticism like asking them to explain themselves.

And always remember the golden rule of office politics, which will stand you in good stead through most work crises: it's not you, it's them.

You know how some people never get knackered, never run out of steam and never lose enthusiasm for a project? Yeah, I'm not that guy. I love my job, but when I'm tired, or stressed out, or doing something I don't want to do, I have to remind myself that I love it. That I'm lucky to be there. And that my job can be as enjoyable as I make it.

But I've had to learn these things the hard way. It took me a decade to realise that the more you put in, the more you get out – but that sometimes you simply can't put in any more without facing diminishing returns. And that's okay too.

In my twenties I constantly felt knackered and stressed, as if I never had enough headspace. Remember the story about the migraine tablets? This happened – as you can probably imagine – when I was going through a tricky work period with a boss I didn't really get (and who, no doubt, didn't really get me either) and very little support. I started getting migraines three or four times a week. They weren't particularly severe but they knocked me out for half a day at a time, putting me further and further behind in a job I already felt as if I couldn't cope with. After a month or so I was spending any time when I didn't have a migraine staring at a computer screen trying to catch up – which gave me more migraines.

In the end I stopped. I went to see a Reiki healer and life coach (don't laugh: it was the best money I've ever spent) who got all Captain Obvious about it and suggested that I made an appointment with my GP, another with an optician, and strongly suggested that I find a way to Chill Out. In the end, I discovered that the migraines were a direct result of too much screen time and not enough sleep (because I was averaging about four hours a night, and spending the rest gazing at a wall, my body coursing with adrenaline and nervous energy).

There were any number of problems with my job scenario, some of which I could control, others that I couldn't. The main one was that I was working in an environment where I could not get the headspace I needed. It was an American company where it was perfectly acceptable to come in at eleven a.m. or not at all (working from home was encouraged and regular hours weren't monitored). However, taking a couple of days off sick and being completely offline or (the horror) going on holiday was completely at odds with the culture. I almost cancelled a two-week holiday to Asia I'd booked before accepting the job because they were so baffled by the concept of twenty days' guaranteed annual leave: in the States there's no minimum statutory paid vacation and, according to the Bureau of Labor Statistics, 77 per cent of private employers offer paid vacation to their employees of ten days per year, on average, after one year of service. In that instance, wiser counsel – my furious travelling companions – prevailed. But I never lost the sense that taking my holiday was the first black mark against my name. An early sign of my lack of commitment to the job, which they were constantly seeking to reaffirm every time I didn't reply to an email quickly enough, or appeared to be thinking about anything that wasn't work.

This creates a culture in which taking time out is frowned upon (American friends frequently talk about not taking their full annual-leave entitlement lest they earn the side eye from their harder working colleagues), and you're expected to be 'always on', no matter how this impacts on your productivity. It was exhausting. The result: I became panicky, dull and uncreative. More concerned with getting through the day and ticking all the 'bare minimum' boxes than doing anything truly great.

But would a few proper days off sick, away from my laptop and my phone, have fixed anything other than my tired eyes? I'm not sure. Part of the problem was that, yet again, I felt a total fraud and completely out of my depth. Now I don't think I was out of my depth: I knew what needed doing – but I was so convinced I shouldn't be there that I couldn't bring myself to do it.

And it turns out that when you feel like that, your body responds in kind. I felt constantly tired, my limbs seemed heavy and cumbersome, and I couldn't think straight enough to make a decision about anything. I can't remember much about huge chunks of that period in my life – which I've since found out is a classic symptom of anxiety.

There are so many reasons why people – women in particular – suffer from anxiety. I don't have an anxiety disorder and I can't imagine how it must feel. But have I been anxious? And has it impacted on how I've felt and behaved in a significant way? Certainly – on numerous occasions.

And for me, it's always come down to one thing: feeling that I'm not a good fit at work. And that I'm not the best possible person on the planet to do that job – which (a) I may or may not be, and (b) what a ridiculous standard to set yourself. It's the doom-laden certainty that I'll mess up monstrously at any moment and my whole life is going to crash around me.

It's moments when I know with absolute certainty (or think I know) that to survive I need to be at the absolute top of my game, defy all expectations (especially my own) and be the best possible version of myself at all times. That's when my body rigs the game against me. And every time I've crashed and burnt, it's because my brain has decided I'm not good enough for the job I'm in, and the rest of me has set out to prove it right.

I'm tempted, for the sake of ease, to describe this as burnout. But I don't think that does justice to the full physical and emotional breakdowns others have gone through at times of emotional strain and crisis. For me a culmination of a couple of months of full-pelt anxiety will be a (sometimes alcohol-fuelled) meltdown and an inability to get out of bed for a couple of days. Or, at worst, a couple of weeks' inertia while I get my head straight and decide what I want to do next. I like to see it as my brain resetting itself, a survival mechanism, so that I don't, in fact, burn out. It's probably best phrased as 'brownout' – an internet-friendly term that, as well as describing a drop in voltage in an electrical supply, can refer to the low-level lethargy and discontent that may come when you're just not feeling it at work. According to some studies, it's on the rise for any number of reasons – from technology (reading your emails in bed is bad, guys) to a reduction in roles with incremental career progress.

Ironically, I get like this when I'm particularly anxious: symptoms of inertia and exhaustion mask the huge levels of anxiety I'm feeling. But, as I've said, there's normally a way out of this. I've worked out the biting point where I need to stop, have a rest, reset my mind and carry on.

But true burnout is more insidious. The phrase was coined in the 1970s to describe the psychological effects of work stress, and is now used to describe everything from a full physical breakdown to that slightly insane feeling you get 2.5 days before you're due to go on holiday and your boss asks you to write a nineteen-page report. But feeling depressed, cynical about a job you used to love, constantly exhausted and falling ill all the time are signs that you could be about to crash.

Author and blogger Laura Jane Williams found this happening to her just as her book, *Becoming*, was published. 'I wasn't myself. I wasn't engaging with books and movies and TV shows – nothing brought me joy or any kind of reaction,' she tells me. 'I was very irritable. Everyone wanted too much of me, whether that was a sixth-former reaching out because they wanted to interview me for their sociology coursework or a friend asking if I wanted to go for drinks tomorrow night. Everything was an inconvenience to me. There was no joy – I had used up all the serotonin in my body. There was none left.'

Laura thinks the pressure of writing such a personal and heartfelt book – and doing it so quickly – contributed to her burning out, as well as a desire to 'appear' successful. 'I think I probably felt a lot of pressure that to do something well is to always be on. I've had to learn to switch off. I think it's a millennium of being scrutinised as a woman. When everything you do is scrutinised how can you not become performative? How can you not pretend to be Someone Who Has It All Together?'

And she's right. The organised, together, quirky, funny, sexy, clever, popular woman we're all meant to be is the vision we're supposed to be presenting to the world, but the pressure of trying to realise that fantasy can be overwhelming.

'It took burning out for me to realise that sometimes I have it together, sometimes I don't, and I'm still worthy. I don't have to perform this role. I feel like I've taken the mask off a bit,' Laura concludes.

But what if you're in that environment all the time? Charlotte, who works in a very Alpha female (and competitive) magazine environment, spoke of the exhaustion of just trying to keep up. 'I find it really tiring. It can make you feel a bit fucking rubbish, like you're not good enough. It can make you feel like you're in competition with each other. Someone will be like "Have you read this article?" and someone else will respond with "No, but have you read this one, or seen this TV show?" And then someone else chips in with "Have you heard this album, or this album, or this album?"'

Assigning Alpha or Beta status to whether we've watched enough of the right box sets, or listened to the right album, sounds ridiculous. Yet we've all done it. I'm constantly feeling disorganised and out of the loop because my film and television consumption are not what they should be. I feel anxious and guilty if I don't read the Sunday papers and an utterly pointless sense of achievement when I manage to get through them. Every time I see someone I know Instagramming from an exhibition I sort-of know I *should* go and see at the weekend (note 'should'), I feel bad. I feel bad that they're sufficiently organised to go out and do stuff at weekends while I'm desperately trying to wash my pants and catch up with work, and then I feel bad because I know that when I do get some down time, I'll probably spend it in the bath, or mindlessly scrolling through my phone, or gazing out of the window.

It's a failure on all fronts for me. Why? Because I haven't sufficiently maximised my leisure time in a way that conforms with a standard absolutely no one, apart from myself, has set for me. Who cares? Why do I care?

And this is why we're all knackered.

Have you noticed that when Barack Obama was president he only ever wore blue or grey suits? No? Well, he did. He explained this choice in an interview with *Vanity Fair* magazine. 'I'm trying to pare down decisions. I don't want to make decisions about what I'm eating or wearing because I have too many other decisions to make.'

Famously, Steve Jobs, the late co-founder and CEO of Apple, always wore a black turtleneck and jeans, while Mark Zuckerberg, owner of Facebook, is rarely seen in anything other than a black hoodie with a grey T-shirt and jeans. Why? Because, like Obama, they want to focus their decision-making energies on the important stuff, not the minutiae of day-to-day living. Decision fatigue exists: studies show that making lots of decisions has a detrimental impact on our willpower. The more decisions we have to make, say, before going out for a drink with a friend after work, the less likely it is that our willpower will hold out: you will make a bad decision (three large glasses of red wine, a packet of salt and vinegar crisps and a box of chicken on the way home). The other way people respond to decision fatigue? They preserve the energy that making another decision would use up by making no decision at all. A study by Jonathan Levav of Stanford and Shai Danziger of Ben-Gurion University, cited in a 2011 article about decision fatigue by John Tierney in the *New York Times*, found that the parole board of an Israeli prison, comprising a judge, a criminologist and a social worker, paroled offenders they saw first thing in the morning 70 per cent of the time, compared with 10 per cent of the offenders they met at the end of the day.

Offenders were much more likely to be paroled in the morning because the board members' minds were fresh and incisive. By the end of the day, when they had used most of their energy, they would deny parole rather than make a bad decision – thereby making none at all. The prisoners hadn't been released, which would have risked them going on a crime spree, but there was still the possibility that they would be paroled at a later date.

Decisiveness is a trait commonly associated with Alphas and strong leaders. I am not very decisive. Or, more accurately, I can be incredibly decisive in the right circumstances, but those circumstances don't come along very often. When I'm feeling low-level harassed (that is, most of the time), I put off making even small decisions, until those small issues become huge, almost insurmountable problems that require much more mental energy to tackle. I'm good at making a decision when I absolutely have to, such as when the now almost insurmountable problem absolutely has to be tackled or when I'm about to go on holiday and stuff just 'needs sorting', or when I have a completely clear head and desk, with no big problems hanging over me. Between those two extremes, when my head is full of the fug of everyday life? I'll put off making a decision and look to maintain the status quo wherever possible.

The female leaders who – outwardly at least – appear the most Alpha to me (and they are often some of the women I admire most) are able to make thoughtful decisions quickly, seemingly without becoming weighed down by them. They don't attribute emotion to decision-making or, indeed, to the decision itself in the way that I do. How do they cut out the crap and focus on the important stuff?

A few years ago, journalist and writer Anna Hart realised she had made her life so busy that she never had time to enjoy any of it. 'I spent my early twenties after I first moved to London accumulating stuff. Clothes and DVDs, yes, but also friends and acquaintances, hobbies, habits like yoga and zumba and other things to occupy my time. This was probably right for me for a time, but one day it hit me that all these things I'd used to build my life were actually holding me back from doing what I wanted to do. This sounds dickish, but I had too many friends – I couldn't see them all and felt like a crap friend to everyone. I spent my nights dashing to two or three drinking sessions, spending way too much time on the tube and not really enjoying any of it. It was the same story with my stuff – my wardrobe was so full I couldn't see those amazing dresses at the back of it. And by trying to cram in yoga, climbing, running, swimming and zumba classes, I never really got good at any of it.

'So I made a decision to simplify my life: I went freelance, immediately cutting out at least three hours of travel every day. My productivity immediately soared, and by biking everywhere rather than taking public transport, travelling was no longer a waste of time, it was exercise and pretty enjoyable.

'I became super-strict about the work events I would go to – I used to force myself to attend them all in case I missed a networking opportunity or whatever. But it took its toll on my energy levels and productivity. Ultimately being pickier about what I attend has definitely improved my career rather than harming it.

'I'm not completely closed to new people, activities and things – that would be a recipe for a joyless life – but I've learnt to accept that time is finite. And doing something new means less time for what you've already got in your life. So it needs to really, really be worth it.'

I love this story because it's a great reminder that our time is precious, and it's our own, yet so many of us give it away to other people without a second thought out of . . . guilt? Obligation?

Anna is a great example of someone who has managed to cut the minutiae out of her day . . . but did you notice that the three other examples I've cited, who have done that with their wardrobes, are men? Because a lot of the crap, whether that's deciding what to wear, working out who can pick up the children from school or finding a meeting room for the client who's coming in, naturally falls on women's shoulders. It's harder to make that big strategic decision about the future of your department if you've already made thirty smaller decisions that day and it's only eleven a.m.

Barack Obama's suit story is a good one: compare that (and that no one had particularly noticed that he only ever wore two suits until he pointed it out) with the scrutiny of his wife, Michelle, as First Lady, particularly her clothes. Arguably the First Lady role, as Michelle Obama understood it, is to be more than a clothes-horse. In her eight years she tackled childhood obesity with her Let's Move initiative, became an advocate for military families, joined the campaign to bring back the Chibok schoolgirls, who were kidnapped in Nigeria, and was a vocal supporter for same-sex marriage. She probably had to make more decisions in any day than most chief executives, and had more important things to think about than whether she was wearing Jason Wu or J. Crew today, but those were still the decisions we judged her on.

Or let's look at the British Prime Minister Theresa May. From the Vivienne Westwood coat she wore to meet the queen when she took office, to her infamous leopard print kitten heels (yes, a pair of kitten heels can be infamous) her clothing choices are scrutinised in a way that her colleagues or rivals rarely are (Jeremy Corbyn's anoraks and Boris Johnson's bicycle clips get noted, yes, but they don't get anything like the same sort of air time). Yes, Theresa May and Michelle Obama have big teams around them, but that doesn't change the fact that they are still, as individuals, expected to make hundreds of decisions every single day. And, unlike the Mark Zuckerbergs and the Steve Jobses of the world, they can't opt out of deciding what they wear, because how they present themselves is a big part of how we judge them.

Obviously, Michelle Obama's Jason Wu dress is the thin end of the wedge. The point is, we all know what happens when you have to make too many decisions each day – your ability to make the big ones becomes impeded. You burn out. And the playing field isn't level: women are expected to make dozens of micro-decisions each day that simply don't trouble most men. And that will impact on our ability to be decisive and thoughtful when we need to be.

And my decision-making, like most people's, is certainly worse when I'm plagued by self-doubt. If I don't believe I'm in the right role, if I don't believe I'm doing a good job, or if I think someone else could be doing it better, then I become much more indecisive because I'm constantly second-guessing myself and trying to work out what a better, more Alpha woman would do in my shoes. The mental energy used up by each decision is equivalent to that which would normally be spent on three. When I feel like that, every decision becomes a series of trade-offs – further zapping my willpower and leaving me feeling stressed and knackered.

A series of fairly heartbreaking studies shows that people living in poverty demonstrate less willpower over time because they constantly have to perform small trade-offs to make their income meet their needs. This constant decision-making makes it harder for them to reserve energy for less important stuff. It's been found that low self-control and low income are linked, but the concept of decision fatigue changes the narrative around this at a fundamental level: it suggests that low self-control is born of circumstance, rather than being its cause.

This also matters in a workplace context: if you're overburdened with decisions, constantly making trade-offs – even if they're just with yourself – and second-guessing everything, your willpower and energy levels will become more depleted. The seeds of self-doubt that have been planted in your brain will flourish, and the more you question yourself, the harder you will find it to be effective.

Writer Daisy Buchanan discovered this when she took on a new role at a magazine she had always adored. She quickly realised it wasn't for her – but couldn't bring herself to make an active decision to quit. 'I felt like I was being crap at work because I was a bad person, and leaving would make me even more of a bad person. By staying I was not making a decision to do anything, and it meant I was in stasis – it was like I'd gone into hibernation and couldn't make a decision about anything.

'It was like every decision I made felt like the wrong one, so I'd try and do the opposite, but that felt wrong too. I was like a tyre that had lost its tread, and not just at work. I got really scared about getting dressed in the morning and deciding what to wear to work, I wasn't sure if I was allowed to leave in the evenings, and there would be meetings where I was never sure if I was supposed to be there or not – and I'd always get it wrong.'

I've definitely experienced this at work too: the worse things get, the harder it is to pull yourself out of that spiral of self-doubt. It becomes utterly exhausting.

Daisy continued: 'My friends said that in this period I seemed really far away, almost like I was medicated – but once I'd handed in my notice, and made the decision to leave, I wrote the freelance piece I'm most proud of. Once I'd done that everything lifted and it was like I was myself again.'

It's hard to discuss burnout, or the modern definition of burnout, without looking at social media a bit more. Not just the expectations it places on us to be perfect and present a certain image, but the impact the very act of being plugged in all the time has on our brain, our cognitive function and our ability to make decisions and implement them effectively (the very definition of productivity at work, surely).

Let's revisit the fictional archetypal successful woman, shall we? Because how she is outside work is as intimidating as her professional life. Yes, she's constantly connected (although she doesn't give the impression that she's a slave to social media, she's far too in control for that) and can demonstrate laser-like focus and an effortless ability to dart from one topic to another, solving problems quickly and incisively, and always able to recall the most obscure but useful statistic or make the most salient argument for her case. But when she's with her friends she's fun and attentive, and when she's with her colleagues, she's absorbed in the task at hand. And she can also explain the story behind every trending topic on Twitter, her every social-media account is updated at entirely appropriate intervals, she's watched every important box set on Netflix, is horrified that you still haven't finished season one of *House of Cards*, and confesses to watching old episodes of *The Hills* as a guilty pleasure when she's hung-over. There's no podcast she hasn't listened to, no album she hasn't heard, no gig she hasn't been to, and no book she hasn't read. Opting out isn't an option.

Has anyone wondered why this woman's brain hasn't short-circuited?

Phrases like 'social-media burnout' and 'information overload' are frequently bandied about to describe what can happen when we're constantly assaulted with information and distractions on social media. But what we're really talking about here is good old-fashioned multitasking on an industrial scale. We absorb so much information on an hourly or even minute-by-minute basis, yet studies have shown that if we don't use it almost immediately, we lose up to 75 per cent from our brains, rendering useless most of the stuff we're bombarded with.

Constant distractions by social media, beeping phones and computers, and colleagues asking you questions are all impeding your ability to get the job done. Glenn Wilson, visiting professor of psychology at Gresham College, London, found that people's problem-solving performance dropped by the equivalent of ten IQ points when they multitasked – and crucially discovered that their stress levels also rose.

Earl Miller, a neuroscientist at MIT and one of the world experts on divided attention, agrees that multitasking isn't the ideal state for the human brain because we're 'not wired to multitask well . . . When people think they're multitasking, they're actually just switching from one task to another very rapidly. And every time they do, there's a cognitive cost.'

So, a lot of the hallmarks of a busy, obviously successful person you see – constantly moving from task to task with seeming ease and unbroken focus – are probably a myth. And the busy Alpha woman who is able perfectly to curate and update her social-media feeds while managing a team of twenty with an iron fist, and nailing her passion project on the side, may be better at creating the impression that she's multitasking than actually doing it (or maybe not doing everything properly).

The problem, according to Dave Crenshaw, author of *The Myth of Multitasking*, is the 'switching cost' – the time taken to switch from one task and refocus on another. 'You take much longer to accomplish things, make more mistakes and increase your stress.'

Professor Wilson also noted that while women were better multitaskers than men, their stress levels rose more significantly than men's when they were forced to multitask – and, of course, multitasking requires constant decision-making, and we all know what that can do. Which begs the further question: if multitasking isn't any good for our brains, what is it doing to our souls?

Here is the headline from one article on the subject from Motherboard, Vice's technology website: 'All of Your Devices Are Bumming You Out'. They were referring to a Michigan State University study, which found that higher media multitasking was associated with higher depression and social-anxiety symptoms, and that 'The unique association between media multitasking and these measures of psychosocial dysfunction suggests that the growing trend of multitasking with media may represent a unique risk factor for mental health problems related to mood and anxiety.' Meanwhile a newer study by the University of Sussex found that social-media multitasking can change the structure of our brains, shrinking the part that processes emotion.

That's why the link between the way we make decisions, our attitudes towards multitasking and the use of social media are all so important in how we measure success. Alpha or Beta, we're setting the bar too high for ourselves in pursuit of a level of perfection it's impossible to emulate. Our brains are capable of amazing things, but when we're constantly trying to work the angle, multitask and make hundreds of decisions each day, all focused around how we're perceived by the wider world, our brains are liable to short-circuit. It's time we gave them – and ourselves – a break and took life one step at a time. That might be the most Beta sentence ever written: after all, stopping, taking a step back and doing nothing is rarely cited as the secret to anyone's success. But it may stop us having a massive meltdown.

Because this culture of competitive perfection and nailing everything doesn't make us the best at what we do. It doesn't make us fulfil our full potential, or be our most creative or our happiest. It dulls sharp minds. It means we spread ourselves too thinly. *And*, despite all of the work, stress and effort, we *still* think everyone else is doing more than us.

And that is the biggest myth of all.

9.

IT'S WHAT'S ON THE OUTSIDE THAT COUNTS (AND WHY EVERYONE'S JUDGING YOU)

'You just know as a black girl that you're not allowed to be outspoken, you just know. When I had my first job I worked for a TV magazine and I learnt very quickly that the girls that were my age who were white were allowed to speak out. But when I did the same, there would be a throwaway comment like "You don't need to have that attitude." That was when I was twenty-one and I just learnt very quickly that I'm not allowed to have the same sort of opinion as my white female counterparts.'

I don't have a silly anecdote about a mishap at work to start this chapter because my experience here isn't that relevant. If we're looking at how race, sexuality, body size, disability or even the way you speak impact on how you're treated in the workplace, then all the cards are in my favour. Anything that's holding me back is internal. It's stuff that's going on in my head. Fear, anxiety or lack of confidence – the things people can't see.

But what if the thing that affects people's perception of you is external? What if it's something you have no control over that impacts on how people perceive you at every level? What do you do then?

'I'm very aware of how much I speak,' says Tobi, in her twenties, the journalist who opened the chapter. 'I am very aware that if I'm in a group setting and it's quite mixed . . .

Let's be real, if I'm in a group setting and it's very white and I'm the only black woman in the room, I don't want to be the woman about whom they say, "Oh, yes, she speaks a lot, she's really loud." I just don't want to be that person, I don't want people to have that memory of me.'

Beverly, fifty-four, works for a large international leisure brand. She's African American and characterises herself as 'driven, determined, very aggressive, focused, data-driven, very intense'.

So, Alpha. Beverly isn't particularly concerned about being considered a tough boss. 'I'm older, I'm African American, I'm female, tall, intense. I'm aggressive, assertive, very direct and specific with my language, I'm experienced, I know what I'm doing, so not only do I have that personality, I have the experience to back it up. So, yeah, it's intense. I imagine working for me is hard.

'One of the things I think I compensate with is that I smile a lot. I'm very happy and tell lots of jokes. I'm always in a good mood for the most part – and even if I'm not actually in a good mood, I'm always "spectacular". I think that people expect me to be angry based on how intense I am so it throws them off when I'm not. Also, I've found that humour and smiles disarm people because the stereotypes of being an angry black female in American culture are very intense.'

Although a classic Alpha, Beverly is aware that for Beta women of colour the challenges are myriad. 'I have a couple of young women who work on my team – they're more Beta than Alpha without question. One of the things I've tried to teach them is to avoid using colloquialisms in their conversations. They're the digital generation and they tend to bring memes to life in their conversation . . . One of them will become very exaggerated with her language, she'll say things like "*Girrrrl*" or "No, ma'am," and I've told her that her personality isn't strong enough to combat the unconscious bias that is associated with her playing that caricature.'

This works on two levels, part of which I can relate to. A trait I see in myself, which feels very Beta, is that I'll sell myself short, or tell a silly joke or story against myself to make other people feel comfortable – even though I might be setting myself up as a buffoon. I undermine myself when I do it. Beverly's employee might be doing the same thing to make other people feel more comfortable, but she is also playing into people's unconscious bias about her. And that's something Beverly feels you need a very strong (Alpha) personality to overcome. 'It's one thing to do that sort of thing in the context of your friends and the people who know you and what you're capable of, but it's another to do that in the workplace, because for women of colour, and women of colour who are Beta, that can torpedo your career. It allows people to paint you into a box and they then begin to have ideas about where you can and cannot excel. If your personality is not strong enough to combat this narrative, then you are limited.'

Beverly's story really does highlight how my agonising over whether I'm Alpha or Beta enough at any given time is very much a white-girl problem. Because although I believe my white male colleagues have more autonomy than I do to be themselves in the workplace, every woman of colour I've spoken to has talked of having far less latitude in the workplace than I do.

In America, the Center for Women Policy Studies found 21 per cent of women of colour surveyed did not feel they were free to be 'themselves at work'. The study also found that more than a third of women of colour – ranging from 28 per cent to 44 per cent – believed that they must 'play down' their race or ethnicity to succeed.

Also in the States, a 2015 study by Catalyst, *Women in S&P 500 Companies by Race/Ethnicity*, found that women of colour make up 0.4 per cent of S&P 500 (Standard & Poors 500: an American stock market index) CEOs, and that only 4.6 per cent of S&P 500 CEOs are women at all. Catalyst also talks about women of colour facing a concrete ceiling rather than the glass one their white female colleagues have to contend with. The difference? It's virtually impossible to smash through, and you can't even see through it.

The issues around gender, race and office politics are complex and myriad. 'When you're in it, it just becomes a case of "How do you survive?"' explains Nicky, who eventually left her job in advertising after she found herself listening to daily instances of casual racism from the rest of the team she was in (which was all white, all male), and felt unable to speak out. 'I did not have the perspective to find the right thing to do. Even when I spoke to my friends about it outside work and they were like "Are you kidding me?"

'But the point when I decided I was not doing this any more was when I thought, If my dad were a fly on the wall of this conversation in this room, and saw me not saying anything he'd be so ashamed. But I felt like I couldn't flag it up because it would be seen as me playing the race card.

It's a ridiculous thing to say because, realistically, there are very, very few instances in which a person of colour would play the race card. It's just not something that you're comfortable doing, it's not an easy go-to option. In the end, I just left.'

Part of the trouble, she feels, is that a lot of the tiny acts of racism she encounters as a woman of colour at work are so insidious – micro-aggressions she's expected to deal with constantly on top of her actual job. 'That's the thing, you never know. But it's like a sixth sense you have in your back, when you can't quite point to what it is but you just know. So that's the thing, you can't quantify it and you can't say what it is.'

Bridget is a freelance writer in her twenties. The prospect of untangling the gender and race politics of an office environment have put her off applying for permanent jobs, even though having a regular job and a steady income appealed to her. 'The friends that I have, women of colour, have all had a lot of issues,' she explains. 'It only really works if you're in a very female-oriented workplace, which is a real privilege. Generally my friends who work in mixed environments find it very, very difficult. Whether they're at the bottom of the ladder and people think they're the cleaning ladies, or if they're somewhere in the middle and they get treated like someone who is brand new.

'My friend said, "I feel like I have to work so hard to prove myself to people who are junior to me." She looks very young – she's thirty-one but could pass for twenty-four – and she's black but didn't go to uni. She said she feels like she has to prove herself so she puts on this aggressive

Alpha role. She's not like that but it's the only way she gets their respect.'

And it's not a trade-off Bridget wants to make. She's also aware that even in the media or the theatre, where people are aware that they should be more diverse, actually putting it into practice is another matter. 'In a space that is very white, like the arts and journalism, people are aware of race problems and, with a few notable exceptions, they broadly want change. So when you're already there, people naturally want to stay in that realm because it makes them feel better. But, if there were ten people on a team then two people would have to leave in order for more diverse people to arrive.'

And the nuances of race and gender in the workplace are intensely complex. Laura, thirty-four, works in tech. She is Chinese, and she feels that, much of the time, this works to her advantage as it plays up to the stereotype that if she's Chinese she must be good with numbers and data: in that context, her face fits. 'I feel like on very rare occasions that I'm just different – but for the last ten years I've managed to embrace it and use it to my advantage.

'When I'm in a room with a group of Caucasian middle-aged men, they don't know what to do with me. I'm "the other". But, on the whole, my experience has been that if you're a woman in tech you're protected, but if you're in an area that's less data- or tech-oriented, if you're in the service industry, for example, then it doesn't work the same way.'

This is what Nikki, a Chinese English woman aged thirty-seven discovered after several years in a customer-service role: 'There was a big difference in my work ethic from that of my white colleagues. I was working silly hours, which they rarely did. People who were less capable than me were promoted above me, and you're not meant to talk about your pay, but I found out they were earning more than me too. One of my friends at work – who was white – kept saying it was a race issue, but I only fully realised it once we got a new CEO in. He was Asian, and all of a sudden I started being invited to more senior strategy meetings, and my hard work started to be recognised. Eventually all those tiny things – being looked over for promotions, other people being promoted above me – clicked. It was a race issue – my face just didn't fit.'

The thing is, everyone should get to say how they're defined in the workplace, not other people, no matter how unconsciously they're doing it. No one's card should be marked the minute they walk through the door. You need to be able to do your job, to speak up in a meeting, to defend yourself and show passion if you want, without someone making a value judgement about you in the process.

For Tobi, her hair is a big part of this – case in point, changing attitudes to women of colour with natural hair. 'At the moment I have quite curly big hair and it's quite a statement, an unapologetic statement. And for a while, I would never have had curly hair like that, I would always have it straight, because it's this whole thing about [how] our hair is politicised, like I'm trying to make this massive statement about being black – it couldn't just be hair. But things have moved on so that now, like if I got a job tomorrow in a mainstream office, I think I could have natural hair, especially in journalism. I think people are over it now. I think people get it more. But rewind four years ago, I was definitely less comfortable having it.'

There's a long and depressing history of black women being disciplined, sent home from work or even losing their jobs over their hair – from the Zara employee in Toronto who was told her box braids were 'unprofessional' to the woman who was told by her London employer to wear a weave because her natural hair was . . . unprofessional. This happens time and time again in office environments, restaurants and even schools. And the word 'unprofessional' is so loaded, isn't it? It implies you're sloppy or lax. Like you just couldn't be bothered to make that bit of extra effort to get your hair all slick and shiny and straight.

But what it really means is 'You don't look the way I think someone who works for me should look.' And how women 'should' look appears to be as Caucasian as possible. This is so far removed from any given person's ability to do their job it's laughable, and yet it persists.

And then there's the clothes we wear, the makeup we may or may not put on our faces, the amount we weigh. Ninety per cent of the time they have no relationship to how we do our job, yet everyone has an opinion on them – and is keen to dish it out like the sagest careers advice you've ever heard.

Bridget used to wear her hair in braids, before deciding to shave her head completely. She said the act itself was freeing – 'It feels liberating. I hated doing my hair. It feels so much nicer not to spend a fortune on getting my hair braided every month.' But it has also had an impact on how she is viewed, and the unconscious bias people have towards her. 'I [now] feel like I'm allowed to wear big bold hoops from my youth again, whereas when I had big hair, words like "ghetto" and "hood" would come to mind. But the image of a woman with their head shaved is more middle class. It's different.'

I've worked at casual, laid-back agencies where I've been told my jeans and trainers weren't appropriate, just as a more senior male colleague emerged from a meeting room with a client in jeans and trainers. I've been told I dress too 'young'. I've been told I look too 'corporate', and I've been told I look 'tired' almost every time I don't wear makeup to work. In fact, I once stopped wearing makeup to work for about three months because I was very busy and tired, and several people asked me if I was 'coping'.

On the other hand, when I 'get it right' that's noted too – and not in the 'women admiring other women's clothes' way. It's more 'I see you've stepped up your game/started wearing mascara again/finally bought a new dress. Got your eye on that promotion, have you?' from a smarmy (male) manager, who tries to read you via your wardrobe choices so he doesn't have to make the effort of actually finding anything out about you.

I do it too. The women I most admire in the office always look fantastic – smart and cool, not too corporate, just the perfect version of who they're trying to be. It's part of why I admire them because to me it's a sign that they've got themselves together, that in the long list of things they've had to remember to do that day, they also pulled out the perfect outfit from their perfectly curated wardrobes. They've done the one last thing, that cherry on top, that screams, 'I'm really professional,' or 'I've got it together,' or 'I make loads of money and am really successful.'

But what I've done – and what we all do to some extent – is go from admiring these women because they have a good eye for nice clothes, great personal style and make an effort to thinking that their appearance is the reason they're great at their jobs.

My boss is pretty kick-ass in most scenarios, and is also very stylish. The two aren't mutually inclusive, but I always secretly think that if I were as good at wearing a blouse as she was, I'd be a bit more kick-ass too.

But what about the guys? Everyone wears clothes, so they have the same problem too, right? Sorry, I'm not buying it. When it comes to men and clothes, there are fewer rules, there's less ambiguity, and less consequence when they get it wrong. If it's a formal working environment they wear a suit, or an open shirt and a jacket, while women periodically grapple with whether or not a trousersuit is a thing. And if it's a casual office . . . Well, I've only ever worked in offices with no formal workwear policy, and while my outfits – and the outfits of my female colleagues – have been commented on or noted on numerous occasions, I've never seen or heard it happen to a man, including the guy who wore flip-flops and shorts to work every day of the year.

As if further proof was needed, a 2017 report by the parliamentary Petitions Committee and the Women and Equalities Committee reveals just how archaic our generalised attitude to what women wear in the workplace still is. As part of the report, MPs spoke to women who had been sent home from work for not wearing heels, told to dye their hair blonde for their jobs, and wear more makeup or more revealing clothes. And, of course, the report unearthed more stories of black women being told to remove their braids or get their hair chemically relaxed, lest they look . . . unprofessional. That word again.

You could argue that women have more choice in terms of what to wear – which in turn gives women more opportunity to get it 'wrong', whatever that means. But, fundamentally, women are judged far more for their appearance than men ever are – from politicians to pop stars.

A 2016 study by the University of the West of Scotland found that when employers look at the social-media profiles of prospective candidates, they're more likely to judge women on appearances and men on content. Researchers asked a group of men and women to look at a series of Facebook profiles and judge each person as a potential candidate for a job.

Dr Graham Scott, who helped to conduct the study, explains, 'When it comes to assessing female candidates, there is a lot of reliance on photographs to judge the qualities of the candidate – this is true regardless of whether it's a man or a woman reviewing the profile. Name is looked at first, then images. Finally, recent posts and friends are looked at. When it comes to assessing a male candidate, both men and women focus on name, profile information, recent posts, and friends.'

And women are more concerned with their external appearance than men because, simply, we are judged far more on how we look than men are. How we look is part of how we're evaluated.

It's like a code we have to unpick: what sort of person does my boss/employer want me to appear to be? How much of my own character or personality can I afford to include before they start to feel uncomfortable? How do I translate this into an affordable, flattering, comfortable wardrobe of clothes I don't hate?

And even if you're willing to go along with it and to play the game, you can't ask. You can't say to your boss, '*Soooo*, Kevin, if I were to dress like a real-life avatar of the woman you imagine is the perfect employee, so as to ensure that you feel comfortable and reassured in my presence, what would that look like?'

That would be a very strange conversation indeed, and would probably result in HR taking you to one side to reiterate that Kevin has never said, on any occasion, that he'd like to conduct an extramarital affair with you. Nonetheless, most of us dress to please our boss, our colleagues, our clients. We dress to make them think we're a safe pair of hands but not too safe, that we get them, but we're also injecting something new into the mix. That we're original, passionate and creative, but not so much as to become a liability.

If I'm being honest, sometimes I enjoy it. If I've got the right thing to wear, that I know I look good in and doesn't give me sweat patches, it boosts my confidence, makes me feel I look the part, as if – for once – I've got the whole package right. I look the part, therefore I am the part. It must be true. I've nailed the cherry on the top.

But I'd say it makes me 2 per cent better at my job. Possibly 5 per cent at an absolute max if I have to do something particularly scary that day.

And this is all great . . . but what if you don't want to wear what other people deem 'stylish', or 'professional', or 'appropriate'?

A few years ago I put on a bit of weight – a couple of stone, so not loads in the grand scheme of things, but enough to take me from averagely slim through to 'Wow, your boobs have got big,' and 'Getting a bit matronly . . .' Before that, I'd considered what I wore in a professional capacity to an extent, but I'd never worried about what I could 'get away with' or 'dressing for my age'. Suddenly these were primary concerns. I felt as if putting on weight was a sign I was getting a bit slobby and lazy (in reality it was mainly a sign that I rarely left my desk), and if I didn't wear the right clothes, people would think I hadn't noticed, or didn't realise, or wasn't trying to do anything about it. Having more flesh on display than usual no longer felt fun or risqué, it felt like an undignified move that would embarrass my colleagues as much as it would embarrass me. People only want to see flesh when it's young and nubile and, well, not very fleshy, you see.

Fashion was out, obviously – I wasn't allowed to do fashion until I bucked up my ideas and trimmed down – so I started wearing 'classic' clothes in muted colours, ostensibly in an attempt to look 'more professional' and 'my age'. In reality, I was making a transition to the person I thought I was about to become: 'the slightly bigger girl who dresses well for her size'.

Just to reiterate, it was two stone. I'm not even that short. It was not a big deal. I wasn't even really overweight on the BMI chart. No one gave a damn except me. Yet something I'd never once considered, my weight, suddenly became of crucial importance at work: it meant I was out of a club I never knew I was a member of – The People Who Just Fit In.

And then there's our voices. We think about what we're saying all the time, but have you ever considered how you're saying it? As much as I hate the way my voice sounds in recordings, I always kind of assume that when I'm talking to someone face-to-face they're more concerned with what I'm saying than how I'm saying it.

But I could be wrong.

There are some aspects of how we speak and how we're judged by it that cut across gender lines (although I still maintain that, as with most things, men have more latitude than women) – the use of slang, swear words or regional accents, for example. How much of an impact these things have is up for debate. A 2013 ITV/Comres study found that eight out of ten employers admitted making discriminating decisions based on regional accents, while 28 per cent of British people feel discriminated against because of how they speak.

Meanwhile a 2015 report from the Social Mobility and Child Poverty Commission found that recruiters favoured people with certain accents over others, regardless of academic merit. Speaking with a Birmingham accent is considered less intelligent and attractive than not opening your mouth.

Dr Alex Baratta from Manchester Institute of Education believes that, while in America regional accents tend to be indicators of race, in the UK it's all about class. In one small study he conducted with trainee teachers, he found that those from the north or Midlands were told to modify their accents far more than those from the south. He also noted that women were asked to modify their accents more than male trainees. Posher accents weren't necessarily a bonus: 'RP [received pronunciation] can be seen as authoritative, posh, educated, but it can also come across as arrogant and stuck-up. It's all about the perception people take from it.'

He's right – although a posh accent still works in your favour in some areas – acting as a signifier of a private school, then an Oxbridge education (the City, the upper echelons of the Tory Party), in other areas, a regional accent might actually work for you.

Louise, thirty-two, flattened her Yorkshire accent when we were at university together in London. She then went to work in PR before becoming a researcher for a Conservative MP. 'I affected my accent a lot at university because most of the people I knew had been privately educated and were really well spoken – I just assumed that's what you were expected to do. It certainly was in PR – even though my accent had all but disappeared by then, the fact that I was "northern" was still commented on.'

Later, when she was working for the MP, she realised that her gender and Bradford background were a bonus: they made her stand out from a sea of posh white men in similar roles. It made her interesting in a world of dull people.

Conversely, my friend Alice, the civil servant I mentioned earlier, was privately educated and thinks her relatively posh accent sometimes works against her in an environment that's (ostensibly) committed to egalitarianism.

But there's one aspect of the voice that is still, for the most part, a female problem: pitch. While Louise spent years thinking about her regional accent and what that would mean for her career, she never considered that the pitch of her voice might cause her a problem. 'I've got a high-pitched voice in a company where only 13 per cent of employees are women – it's definitely noted,' she says. 'I'm fine when people get to know me, but I think it really impacts on how people see me at first – I've caught someone almost unthinkingly going to mimic me on more than one occasion. It's definitely been noticed in the business – I'm being sent on a Speaking With Impact course soon, not something any of my male colleagues have ever been asked to do.'

Scientists reckon that the pitch, timbre, volume, speed and cadence of your voice have a massive impact on how convincing you are and how people judge your character. And if you're high-pitched, or even sound 'too feminine', you're judged more harshly. A study by scientists from Northwestern University, the University of Colorado and Tilburg University in the Netherlands found that a more feminine voice is perceived to be 'less competent' than a male voice, while research suggests that both men and women prefer people with masculine voices in leadership roles.

And let's not forget vocal fry.

You'll have heard vocal fry, even if you don't realise it. Vocal fry is 'the lowest vocal and is produced through a loose glottal closure which will permit air to bubble through slowly with a popping or rattling sound of a very low frequency'. It's that low, slightly growly affectation that you'll sometimes hear in American women (the Kardashians are prime offenders, if that's the right word). In 2011, a group of scientists at New York's Long Island University recorded thirty-four different women speaking. Two speech pathologists listened to the recordings in search of instances of vocal fry, which featured in two-thirds of them. Hardly a rigorous study, but it spawned a series of articles reporting that vocal fry was (a) really annoying, and (b) on the rise among young women.

The perceived problem with it seems to be that it has Valley Girl-esque connotations, making the speaker sound less bright than she would otherwise, and that it's seen as very much an affectation – something women put on to sound more attractive? Less decisive? Certainly more Beta.

On an episode of the podcast *This American Life*, presenter Ira Glass discusses the issue, noting that while listeners used to write in to radio shows to complain about female presenters using the word 'like', and up-speak (ending a sentence so that it sounds like a question), they now complain about vocal fry. But it's totally gendered: no one is complaining about any of the affectations found in male voices in the same way.

Incidentally, as an article in website Mental Floss points out, linguist and philosopher Noam Chomsky has a pretty bad case of vocal fry, and no one's moaning about that because he's Noam Chomsky.

It's also an age thing. Glass spoke to linguist Penny Eckert, who had conducted a study in which she asked people to rate a radio presenter with vocal fry on how authoritative they sounded. Those under forty thought the presenter sounded authoritative; those over forty did not.

The Society of Teachers of Speech and Drama even describes vocal fry as a speech impediment, with their chairperson saying, 'It seems extraordinary that, having fought hard for the right to be heard, women risk not being listened to, or taken seriously, by adopting a speech impediment – one that is at best laughable, at worst vocally damaging.' It doesn't seem to have occurred to them that if young women aren't being heard it's because people aren't listening properly.

It should go without saying that there's far more value in what people say than how they say it, just as there's far more value in the work you produce than the colour of your skin or your skirt. Yet it all adds up. It all counts towards that one big impression you're making in the workplace so that people can mentally place you in the most convenient box without the effort of having to get to know you. 'Ball-breaker', 'pushover', 'maternal', 'aggressive', 'difficult', 'emotional', 'bitch'.

You can control what you do or say, but how you present yourself, the impressions people are gaining of you day in, day out, are less easy to get a handle on. Everyone wants to belong in the place where they work, and fit. But what if the only way you can fit is to be less weird? Less passionate? Or to stop wearing bright colours, lose weight or wear a weave?

'Fit in or fuck off,' as one of my old bosses used to say, about anyone who didn't really 'get' our company's ethos or culture. He wanted to work with people who thought like him, had the same values as him – and looked like him.

But if fitting in is all about looking and sounding like everyone else, then, as I get older, I know which option I'm going to take.

10.

A: CRIPPLING ANXIETY

The first time I had to chair an event in front of a room of people (probably no more than fifty, so relatively small) should have been easy. It was an 'in conversation' session with a highly experienced, professional woman, who's widely respected across the industry. I also know her personally. True to form, she was fantastic, self-assured, and completely knew what she was doing. I, on the other hand, was a complete mess. I was stuttery, rambling and a little bit drunk (it was an evening event and they'd been serving wine for a couple of hours). It was like that first team meeting when I became an editor all over again. I lost my train of thought, trailed off mid-sentence, and had absolutely no connection with the audience (who were all rooting for me to succeed, which made the whole thing worse). I was so panicked that I lost all sense of why I was there and the story I was trying to tell. My fight-or-flight instinct had kicked in and I just wanted to get off the stage as quickly as possible.

My friend was fantastic. Sensing my discomfort, she launched into a series of juicy anecdotes, which required very little prompting from me, and everyone in the room lapped it up (apart from me: I was desperately trying to pretend I was on Mars).

My friend was born to be on that stage. She was relaxed, funny and self-deprecating. She was confident, had presence and instinctively knew how to connect with the audience. She could talk in detail about her area of expertise without notes or losing track of what she was saying. I looked like I'd rented the stage via a dodgy sublet that I couldn't get out of.

Nothing terrible happened – it was only a small event, no one was filming it and we certainly weren't saving lives, but I was rubbish and came away from the whole thing feeling bruised. Even worse, to anyone watching, I was wildly unconvincing as an editor – a role in which I'm meant to demonstrate authority and confidence, connect with people and tell a compelling story. And I had failed on every front.

A year ago, I had to do a talk. This time I had to present to several hundred people for twenty minutes. I was nervous beforehand, sure (full disclosure: I got total tunnel vision thirty seconds before going on stage), but I got through it, and a few people even came up to me at the end and told me how much they'd enjoyed it. I'm not saying people are now queuing round the block to hear my *bons mots*, but I'm basically fine. That's for two reasons. First, I've made myself stand on stages and talk to people far more frequently than I'd like to – I've taken myself out of my comfort zone on purpose because I know it's the only way I'm going to get better at something that I have to be decent at for my job. But I've also learnt to be honest about my strengths and weaknesses, and thought a bit more creatively about how they can work for me.

I'm far better when someone else is asking the questions,

and tapping out a rhythm in my head keeps my breathing regular and me focused on what I'm trying to say. And memorising what I want to say so that it's imprinted on my brain is crucial, because if I only half know something, or if I have to search around for a piece of information when I'm already feeling panicked, I can guarantee that my mind will go blank.

So, I've learnt how to fake it, but I'll never be a natural public speaker, and it used to go wrong when I pretended otherwise, tried to wing it, didn't prepare properly, or give myself enough time to calm down beforehand.

My point is, you may be able to fake some Alpha behaviour for a twenty-minute slot on stage, for a few hours or days or, in some cases, months, but it all unravels eventually. 'Fake it till you make it' is great advice for when you've got to suck it up and do something that terrifies you – and pushing ourselves out of our comfort zone can sometimes be as rewarding as it is challenging. But what if the role you're in requires you to fake who you are just to get through the day? You've either got to change how the role works for you or find a new one.

When Mary joined the civil service's Fast Stream programme in the 1960s, she had to learn pretty quickly how to fake it. 'I was put in charge of a team of middle-aged men when I was in my mid-twenties – all old suits. Even though I was terrified inside, I told them all, in no uncertain terms, that I was in charge. I've always been able to front it out when I've had to.' Mary had quickly realised that in such a highly dogmatic, masculine world, the only way to get the job done was – in her words – to 'front it out'.

But even though she became adept at exerting her authority when necessary, she discovered that 'faking it' as a matter of course had its limitations when she took over the administrative management of a hospital for a short period: 'The twenty or so consultants were some of the most difficult people I've ever had to deal with – they all behaved like they were God. The whole time I was there, I had to be as difficult as they were in order to get anything done. I could do it, but I hated it – it made me miserable.'

Everyone I've spoken to believes that too much 'faking it' is bad for you – it's bad for your mental health and general sense of wellbeing, and it also makes it impossible for you to demonstrate any semblance of authenticity, which, as we're always being told, is everything.

But what if being authentic means revealing to the world that you're terrified? Or wildly out of your depth? Won't that just lose you credibility? Or is our professed attraction to authenticity simply a way of keeping ourselves in our comfort zones?

There are different views on the psychological impact of constantly being inauthentic. One 2015 study by psychological scientists at Northwestern University, Harvard Business School and Columbia Business School suggested that inauthenticity doesn't just make us feel uncomfortable but as if we've been morally compromised – 'Feeling inauthentic is not a fleeting or cursory phenomenon – it cuts to the very essence of what it means to be a moral person,' explains Maryam Kouchaki, of Northwestern. The scientists speculated that being inauthentic may have similar psychological consequences to overtly lying or cheating.

Faking it all day is said to be more stressful than we

realise. LinkedIn influencer Annie Murphy Paul writes on the site:

> This kind of faking it is hard work – sociologists call it 'emotional labour'. It's psychologically and even physically draining; it can lead to lowered motivation and engagement with work, and ultimately job burnout.
>
> Having to act in a way that's at odds with how one really feels, eight hours a day, five days a week (or longer), violates the human need for a sense of authenticity. We all want to feel that we're the same person on the outside as we are on the inside, and when we can't achieve that congruence, we feel alienated and depersonalised.

Similarly, a study by Alex Baratta from the Manchester Institute of Education found that when people modify their accent, which Baratta feels is common practice in the UK due to 'negative class-based assumptions regarding regional accents in particular', this is not a neutral act. Instead, he found that a third of those studied felt that in modifying their accent – and, as a consequence, their fundamental identity – they were 'selling out'. Faking it didn't sit all that comfortably with them.

So, being inauthentic isn't necessarily great for your brain, or your happiness levels – although let's not discount the serious satisfaction that can be gained from totally fronting something out and it actually working. I still give myself a mental high five when I think about that talk I did. But if I'd been my most authentic self I'd have either stuttered my way through the whole thing or hidden in the toilets. Putting on a face got me through it and allowed me to communicate a big idea to an audience of people I wanted to hear about it. So there's that.

In a 2013 *Harvard Business Review* article, Professors Rob Goffee and Gareth Jones explain why they think authenticity is one of the most important traits for a good leader to have: 'Simply put, people will not follow a leader they feel is inauthentic.' But, more than that, they discovered that the key to happier, more productive staff was an organisation that was authentic in terms of how it was run, and allowed its employees to be true to themselves. They cite research which found that those who feel able to express their authentic selves at work exhibit higher levels of organisational commitment, individual performance and the propensity to help others.

However, as Goffee and Jones point out, very few organisations are able to do this effectively, because other things, like offering people clear career paths, traditional hierarchies or appraisal systems, get in the way. Basically, all the stuff that keeps companies ticking along from a human-resources perspective is at odds with the laudable aim of promoting individual authenticity.

Nonetheless, large organisations, from Waitrose to Apple, still aim to promote individualism because that's where the good ideas come from. Whether it's a data analyst who can number-crunch like no one else, a genius news reporter who can sniff out a great story first, or a visionary creative director who puts the competition in the shade, our talents are part of who we are. The stuff we're good at – really good at – is in our DNA. 'Authenticity' as a buzzword is in danger of being overused to death (certainly in this chapter) but the idea of doing what you're best at, in a way that makes you happy, for an organisation you believe in and whose success is linked to yours is simply the recipe for happiness at work, isn't it?

And it sells. The term 'post-fact world' is more overused now than 'authenticity' but it describes a world in which politicians, news outlets, a blogger or a member of the public can present their version of the truth as fact, and people will be influenced – whether they believe the 'facts' presented to them or not. In a mid-year report in the run-up to the 2016 US presidential election, PolitiFact, a fact-checking outlet in Florida, estimated that 78 per cent of Donald Trump's claims were 'mostly false' or worse. Yet that wasn't enough to stop people voting for him – because what he was saying was less important than the general sense voters got that he was authentic, unvarnished, real.

And it didn't end there. When Trump's press secretary, Sean Spicer, claimed that the president's inauguration drew in the 'largest audience to ever witness an inauguration', a claim that was demonstrably false, all of these discrepancies were explained away by the president's counsellor Kellyanne Conway as 'alternative facts'.

Basically they were lies, but we now exist in a world where the president's press secretary telling outright falsehoods in a press briefing is acceptable, because the broader idea, that Trump and his team are 'authentic' and 'say it like it is' (or, in this case, isn't), counts for more.

At the other end of the spectrum, you have only to look at the stratospheric rise of the vlogger industry. Beauty vlogger Zoella is said to be worth £3 million net, and in 2016 YouTube was estimated to be worth $86.22 billion.

Many of the most prominent – and profitable – bloggers are young people who started making videos at home, from home beauty tutorials to general updates about their lives and lifestyles. It's simple and it sells.

So what's the appeal? It's the A word again – authenticity. Zoella talking about how she struggled with panic attacks seems far more compelling, and real, to young people than Gwyneth Paltrow explaining why she steams her vagina. 'Realness' sells, especially for millennials. If you're discussing every aspect of your life with your mates, blogging about your anxiety to your followers or Snapchatting while you floss your teeth, why wouldn't you expect to be yourself in the workplace?

Goffee and Jones's article on authenticity was written in 2013 and was noteworthy at the time. But that was before 'authenticity' became a buzzword used to describe everyone from Adele to Nigel Farage. But has it been overused to the point at which it's lost all meaning?

Because that's what we do, isn't it? We take a concept or an idea, and we flog it to death until it ceases to mean anything, or until it starts to mean the opposite of what we originally intended. Is that what we've done here? Is authenticity at all costs just another dogmatism to be avoided? Or a cop-out for people looking for a reason not to push themselves?

In January 2015, the *Harvard Business Review*'s cover feature for that issue was 'The Paradox of Authenticity'. The author, economist and leadership guru Herminia Ibarra re-examines whether authenticity really is all, particularly where leadership positions are concerned. She points out that those in leadership positions have to move out of their comfort zones and push themselves. During those transition periods, being authentic isn't always the smartest move, yet when we're uncertain, we often retreat to what's familiar in order to protect our identities. 'Because going against our natural inclinations can make us feel like impostors, we tend to latch on to authenticity as an excuse for sticking with what's comfortable,' she explains. 'But few jobs allow us to do that for long, and that's doubly true when we advance in our careers or when demands or expectations change.'

Ibarra identifies several key reasons why authenticity isn't always the best route to take. Apart from anything else, our authentic self is constantly evolving and changing. And pushing ourselves out of our comfort zones is part of this. Despite all natural inclinations to the contrary, I'm certainly less wary of confrontation than I was, say, three years ago. Circumstances have changed and I've had new challenges to respond to so I've learnt different skills, but also it can be easier and more effective to change your style to get things done than to expect people, or the task you're facing, to mould around you. So, because I'd always hated and feared confrontation, I avoided it like the plague until I realised I'd wasted time and energy in not confronting problems that wouldn't go away – and were getting bigger. Confronting issues as soon as they arise takes a lot of effort on my part – my natural inclination is to ignore or smooth over the bad stuff – but it's sometimes the right thing to do, so I try to make myself do it.

But the idea that your authentic self changes over time is interesting. I would always have characterised my friend Catherine, a former colleague, as an Alpha. And until recently she would have agreed with me. So what's changed?

Motherhood. Or, to be more specific, it was what happened when she went back to work. 'I work part time now and can't – don't want to – put in the hours some of my colleagues do. As a result I've had to become more Beta, let stuff go and take a step back, because it would drive me mad otherwise.'

We'd all like to think that who we are is who we are, and that's that. But external circumstances change our attitudes and our approach to life, and we change too. We aren't one person all of the time, for all of our lives, and by sticking too dogmatically to who our authentic self is, and by staying in our comfort zone, we risk stunting our development.

Another issue with true authenticity lies with our private sense of self: we still need to have one, and throwing ourselves completely open to our colleagues is probably as dangerous as behaving like a completely fictionalised version of ourselves when we're with our colleagues. 'Being utterly transparent,' Ibarra notes, 'disclosing every thought and feeling, is both unrealistic and risky.'

She also points out that cultural norms change from country to country, so if your authentic self is bold and brash, and you find yourself doing business in, say, Asia, where modesty is favoured, it would make sense to adjust your approach accordingly.

Then there's the issue of selling yourself within your organisation. If you're the sort of person who feels your work should speak for itself, you may find doing the jazz-hands aren't-I-great dance to your boss's boss's boss distasteful and inauthentic. But if that's the only way to get your new project signed off, or to get the extra funding you require, surely a bit of inauthentic jazz-handing is worth it.

It's about pay-off, really, isn't it? If you know who you are, what your limits are, and what you want to get out of a role, then inauthentic schmoozing is fine: chances are, you'll emerge with your morality intact.

But no one wants to spend eight hours a day playing a part, and no one wants to think that their partner or best friend wouldn't recognise them if they saw them in the office. I've touched on social media a lot, and that's not really what this chapter is about, but I've always been struck by the contrast between some of the intimidating (read: focused and scarily efficient) work people I know in a professional setting and their social-media personas. They might be known for making four interns cry, but they have friends, and a partner, and children, none of whom appear to be particularly wary of them. Obviously they're just very good at coming to the office with their work head on and leaving it at the door when they go home. But isn't that, in itself, a bit knackering?

I guess it depends on what's required of you. I spoke to Suzanne, a female barrister in her thirties who, at home, 'defers to the needs of the household' but simply has to be more assertive at work to get the job done. 'I'm decisive and a "leader" at work because that is the nature of the job. At work I often think I'm the best qualified to answer. At home I think my view is just one view.'

That's something I hadn't considered until she said it. For me, authenticity is easier to find because I work in an environment that is relatively relaxed, not massively corporate, and broadly encourages creativity and individualism. When your working environment is either a courtroom or legal chambers, of course you're going to be different from how you are at home – they might as well be different worlds.

And then there's the stuff you don't want anyone to know about at work because you think it will change how they see you. When I asked female friends what they like to keep separate from work, some people mentioned their spirituality or religion; others talked about their relationships, their sexual orientation, their financial status or their children. Everyone had different reasons for doing so, but broadly it always boiled down to the same thing: not everything is for public consumption.

Eddie Erlandson, co-author of *Alpha Male Syndrome*, believes that faking an Alpha personality in the workplace is a mistake, but that there are benefits to developing 'alpha personas' where necessary. 'Your greatest impact as a person and as a leader is authenticity and I have what I call "alpha personas" – some of those people who can take on an acting role, and some of them can do it quite well.'

Eddie talks about how his wife and co-author, Kate Ludenham, was able to do this: 'Kate is an Alpha, she is a very evolved one, but when she was head of HR she had a huge male alpha team and she decided that if she was going to be heard in senior leadership meetings, she would have to raise her voice, lean forward, and occasionally slap her hand on the table. So she practised it. It didn't change her but it did allow her to get to the table and in the conversation.'

You don't have to become a parody of yourself, but if you're going to do that scary meeting, or give that presentation, and you can tweak your delivery style to make you feel better about the whole thing, or more in control, why wouldn't you? This isn't about ensuring you fit in by behaving in a certain way, or about making other people feel comfortable by adjusting your behaviour. It's about doing what you need to do to get through something that makes you uncomfortable.

But is it harder for women in the workplace to be authentic than men?

There is some evidence to suggest that women are better suited to adopting an authentic leadership style than men because they tend to be more collegiate and empathetic. However, psychologists Margaret M. Hopkins and Deborah O'Neil believe that it's harder for women to be authentic, particularly in masculine corporate environments. In their 2015 article 'Authentic Leadership: Application to Women Leaders', they identified three reasons why the concept of authentic leadership, as it's currently understood, is gendered, and therefore harder for women to achieve. First, 'masculine leadership behaviours such as assertiveness and competitiveness remain the norm', so women are either expected to behave in as masculine a way as possible or go against leadership norms. Second, and as I've already said, most companies have an organisational structure that is designed for men. When we talk about authenticity at work, we're often talking about authenticity in a male structure, as Hopkins and O'Neil go on to explain:

Even the most progressive modern organizations have been created by and for men, and thus tend to have systems, policies, norms, and structures that favour the male life experience. Behaviours and values regarded as the norm at work tend to favour traits and characteristics traditionally associated with maleness and to undervalue traits and characteristics traditionally associated with femininity.

And, finally, discussion of authentic leadership assumes that the influence an authentic leader has is a one-way street. But you can't adopt an authentic leadership style if the people who work for you simply refuse to respond.

For Naomi, the thirty-three-year-old project manager who works in construction, it's hard to make her desire to be authentic at work into a reality. 'I am a lot more reserved at work than I am at home. I try to control my emotions, including my reactions and facial expressions, as I find being vulnerable in the office is looked down on rather than respected. I have been working on closing the gap to try and be my more authentic self at work, but it is difficult.'

But is authenticity always better? Another woman I spoke to said she embraced the separation between her home and work life. 'They need to be separate to keep things in perspective and alive in both worlds.'

Careers coach Corinne Mills agrees that our authenticity shouldn't compromise our professionalism, although she also feels that it still needs to exist in some form. 'You're a version of your authentic self at work – you don't want to bring all sides of yourself to work because that's not appropriate. The difference in a work scenario is you're expected to have emotional control, at home not so much.'

But although she advocates a decent amount of professional distance from your work colleagues, to ensure professionalism when you're in charge, she thinks being fundamentally authentic in terms of your values is crucial. Because doing what we perceive to be the right thing and doing what's right for our employers isn't always the same. 'If your authenticity is stretched so tight it's going to snap at any moment then it's not the right job for you.'

So where does that leave us? Facing emotional ruin as we try to negotiate a working world that would really rather we were a slightly different type of person? Constantly seeking and failing to find a modicum of that all-important authenticity lest we come across as too soft or too much of a bitch, too sappy or too cold?

I believe it's about self-protection – in every sense. Protect who you are and what you cherish, and don't let what you do for a living eat away at those things. Do what you have to do to protect yourself, even when you have to do things that make you feel tense, nervous or wildly out of your comfort zone (because we all do: it doesn't mean you're bad at your job, it means you're being brave and taking on something new. So give yourself a little high-five for that).

And protect what you do for a living, and what you love about it. Everyone I spoke to who truly felt they had found a way to be authentic at work had done so because they loved most of their job, if not every element of it. And they were committed to the end goal, whatever that was. Because if you truly believe in making something happen, it becomes that little bit easier to be true to yourself in the process.

11.

BE THE ROBIN TO HER BATMAN: HOW TO DEAL
WITH YOUR ALPHA BOSS

I've realised that during some of the happiest points in my career I've had an Alpha (female) boss: I'm always happiest when someone else is taking control of the situation while I do what I'm told. I was also an insanely obedient child – make of that what you will.

When I described in the Introduction what I would view as a classic Beta, I was almost entirely describing myself. And this has always seemed to make me good at dealing with Alpha women. I'm a good sidekick: I'll always help to realise someone else's ambition even if it's at odds with my own – if that's what it takes to keep the peace (this isn't necessarily a good thing) – and I find relinquishing control and ultimate responsibility to someone else ultimately quite freeing. It makes me more creative, gives me more headspace.

There aren't many things in life I'd actively boast about (classic Beta there, y'all), but that's one of them. I don't feel threatened by Alpha women because it's like comparing apples and oranges – we're operating on totally different planes, and unless they're just wrong about something, I'm generally happy to buy into someone else's vision of how stuff should be done and fit in to make that work. Cog in the machine, that's me.

But what if your Alpha boss is a total nightmare? What

if your innate Beta-ness is overridden by your desire for control, or your fear that a certain idea or project is going in totally the wrong direction? What if you unwittingly find yourself in a weird power battle with your Alpha boss and don't want to be, but she's really into it so you'll have to continue to glare at each other across meeting rooms and say things like 'Yes, Pamela, I see your point, but strictly speaking I'm not sure if this issue is in your jurisdiction,' until she gets bored and goes off to terrorise someone else?

When one of my friends, Harriet, got her first proper job, in PR, after uni, I didn't see her for a couple of months. When we finally got together for a drink, she was a shadow of her former self. She'd dropped a dress size, had dark circles under her eyes and could barely speak because her mouth was covered with ulcers. The problem? Her new boss was an unreasonable lunatic (I'm paraphrasing) and despite my friend's best efforts (she's a natural people-pleaser), nothing she did was ever right for the woman, who sent her on pointless errands across London at five minutes to six on a Friday evening, gave her piles of work she had no idea how to do (or any time to do it in) and constantly told her she was useless. My friend responded by doing everything she could think of to make her happy. She tried to make herself as likeable as possible so her boss could have no reason to be affronted by her very presence. She did everything that was chucked at her, plus more, and it didn't work – in fact it enraged her boss. In the end she realised she was about to have a nervous breakdown and quit.

I wonder if another tactic would have worked better.

When you're a Beta woman, with an apparently Alpha boss, your first instinct might be to give them exactly what they say they want (mine certainly is). But this woman wasn't an Alpha boss who knew what she wanted, and demanded a lot from her team. She was newly promoted from her own graduate job, on a power trip, and took far more pleasure in terrorizing the intern than any sane person would. In fact, looking back ten years on, she probably should have been sacked for her behaviour. But if you're a Beta, especially when you're new to the working world, everyone with a loud voice and decisive manner can come across like an Alpha boss who knows what they're talking about. But working out the difference between a bully and an Alpha is the key to being a successful Beta. Had my friend seen her boss for what she was – a bully – she might have responded differently. Or maybe not: standing up to bullies isn't easy.

But just because you're not thumping your fist on the table, speaking up the loudest in meetings or kicking off every time you get your own way, it doesn't mean you're a pushover. One of the most important parts of being a successful Beta is knowing when you're being taken for a ride and having the confidence to speak up and do something about it – even when that goes against every grain in your body.

According to careers coach Corinne Mills, the relationship between your Beta personality and your Alpha boss should be harmonious – that's why you're there. 'In some respects, they've probably chosen you because you're Beta and because they think you're going to be complementary to them.' But, obviously, there are pitfalls, especially when you're a people-pleaser with a demanding boss. 'You just have to be careful if they become unreasonable – we've all had Alpha bosses where there's some power play going on for the sake of it. You have to find a way to let them know you're not in competition with them, to let them know you're there to support them, that you're not there to oust them from their job and you want them to be successful.'

This chapter is looking at how to deal with your female Alpha boss, who may or may not be lovely: it isn't about pitting women against each other. Equally, if you're Beta, this isn't about suppressing your own hopes, desires and ambitions for your job in favour of someone else's. But we all do things differently, and work towards success differently, and we need to get better at acknowledging that: it will make us all enjoy our jobs and careers a lot more in the long run.

We're not very good at talking about women in charge without resorting to broad-brush caricatures. Advice on how to deal with an Alpha female boss often won't tell you how to cope with a powerful and decisive woman, who knows what she wants. Instead, it will – unhelpfully and reductively – be about how to deal with your 'bitch boss' or lament that she's allowed to be your boss at all.

The reality, of course, is far more nuanced and, regardless of whether we're an Alpha or a Beta woman, we all want to do a job that we're fulfilled by and care about. And if you're anything like me, you still want your thoughts and ideas considered properly. You just don't want to have to shout to get them across. How do you do that when your boss is a through-and-through Alpha whose default position is to steam forward with her own ideas, much in the same way as it's your default position to do what you're told? You need to understand what motivates her.

Executive coach and HR consultant Tania Hummel once worked with a chief executive and an MD, whose wildly different approaches to management meant they kept clashing. This is about a man and a woman, not two women, but I love this story because it demonstrates just how different Alphas and Betas can be. It also shows how a Beta isn't always the pushover sidekick and the Alpha isn't always the shouty bitch. They are literally just two different ways of working.

'She had been mentored by a boss who was very like her,' explains Tania of the chief executive. 'She was all about the vision and so was her old boss. But her new MD was very down to earth.

'When she'd worked with her old boss she could bound into his office with all of her ideas and say, "Let's do this," and he would say, "Yeah, let's do this," and they would bounce the ball around. Nothing needed to come of it, but they'd both be satisfied that they'd had that exploratory need fulfilled.

'But when she tried to do the same with this new MD, who was reporting in to her, she would bound into his office with her latest idea, he'd be surrounded by stuff to do and he would go, "Why are you here? We're supposed to meet next Tuesday. Can't you see I'm busy? Do you want me to drop everything to follow this?"'

You can see where the clash lay – but it came from a failure to understand each other's approach rather than a fundamental difference in opinion. 'It's, like, she'd come to him with her ball to play with him [her MD],' Tania continues, 'and he'd say, "What are the rules of the game? This is not scheduled," put the ball down and walk off the pitch until she'd met his requirements.'

Obviously this was a problem because (a) she was his boss, and (b) he failed to realise that she needed to discuss her ideas and have them acknowledged. Bringing them to fruition was the next step – which was what he was preoccupied with. But she was far more concerned with having her ideas discussed in that moment.

Once the pair understood where each other were coming from, their working relationship became much easier. And that is why finding a way to understand your boss's perspective and approach is crucial – even if it varies wildly from yours.

I think, in many ways, Alpha women are easier bosses than Alpha men because they *tend* to be more evolved and more emotionally intelligent than their male counterparts, which makes sense – Eddie Erlandson, co-author of *Alpha Male Syndrome*, described (most) Alpha women's approach to management as akin to a 'velvet glove', and they are said to be less likely to indulge in 'risky' behaviour (as in risky to the business) than their male counterparts. This means that most of the Alpha women I've dealt with have at least attempted to see things from my perspective as much as I've tried to see things from theirs. It doesn't matter how different you are, as long as you both understand your respective roles in the skit.

But what about Queen Bee Syndrome? That's a thing, right? People are always banging on about it as the reason why there are still, relatively speaking, so few women in senior business roles.

The theory, developed in 1973 by three (male) researchers, G. L. Staines, T. E. Jayaratne and C. Tavris, hypothesises that so few women exist in senior positions because those who do make it to the top pull the ladder up with them – thus making it harder for others to succeed. Obviously it's all our fault. Women, eh? A Canadian study from 2008, which found that women with female supervisors had more depression, headaches, heartburn and insomnia than those with male bosses, seems to back this up.

But the reality, of course, is a little more complicated than that.

Yet another study from 2015 suggested that Queen Bee Syndrome as a phenomenon doesn't exist. Research by Columbia Business School found that companies with a female chief executive were more likely to have women in senior management roles. However, in those cases women were facing an unofficial quota: once a woman reached a senior management position (not chief executive), it became 51 per cent less likely that another woman would follow. The implication is that the one woman who makes it to the top is seen as legitimising the business's attempts at diversity, and that's that.

The research team explained: 'Women face an implicit quota, whereby firms seek to maintain a small number of women on their top management team, usually only one. While firms gain legitimacy from having women in top management, the value of this legitimacy declines with each woman.'

The problem isn't other women, it's men (or, at least,

the institutional misogyny that still pervades in plenty of large organisations). But another study also suggests that something more complex is going on: when women with low levels of gender identification – who feel their gender is irrelevant to their role – face gender bias, they attempt to get over this obstacle by setting themselves apart from other women. This may be by displaying typically masculine behaviour or putting down other women.

But the point – and this is crucial – isn't that this is inherently female catty behaviour: it's that this is how some women end up responding to a masculine environment that devalues women. It's the system that's the problem. When there's only one seat at the table for All Women, and you've got it, you want to protect it. You can't have a system that allows one woman at a time to succeed, then act surprised when women start vying to be that One Woman.

Pamela Stone, professor of sociology at Hunter College, New York, agrees that Queen Bee Syndrome is a symptom of a certain workplace culture: 'In the old days, when we used to talk about the Queen Bee Phenomenon, the sense was that the women who made it to the top were basically men, in that they were male identified: they weren't changing culture because it worked for them – their attitude to other women was "If I can do it, why can't you?"

'There was this notion that women in this position would see other women as competition so they wouldn't necessarily be helpful. The chance of any women making progress was so low that it created a hyper-competitive environment among women.'

But as the culture around the workplace (slowly) changes,

Professor Stone believes that the Queen Bee is becoming even less relevant as a cultural phenomenon. 'Now, as we see progress and we see more and more women [in senior positions], it's still competitive as you get higher up, but it's a little bit less sharp-elbowed. We're starting to get research that says the more women you get in leadership positions, it does appear that these organisations create cultures that are a little bit more family-friendly, for example. So you hope that we are in a different era now and women can be a bit more assertive about creating a culture that reflects women's values – not just the Alpha values.'

'Queen Bee Syndrome' is a horrible term for a phenomenon that's been woefully misunderstood. But is it surprising? What do you think would happen if the tables were turned and blokes were given one opportunity in twenty to sit on the board or get the corner office? Within hours it'd be a cut-price version of *Gladiator*. Although the mental image of a bunch of middle-aged wannabe chief executives battling it out in the amphitheatres of Surrey in their vests isn't, admittedly, a great one.

But that's not really the point, is it? The point is, when women are given the latitude to do so, studies suggest that they are active and successful mentors for other women. One survey of high-potential leaders showed that 73 per cent of the women who are developing new talent are mentoring women, compared with 30 per cent of men who are developing talent. When women work with a higher proportion of women they experience lower levels of gender discrimination, and when they have female managers they report having more family and organisational support than when they have male supervisors. And as any number of different studies demonstrate, the more women in management positions, the smaller the gender pay gap.

The Queen Bee Syndrome, as it's described to us, is a myth, a damaging one as it feeds into any number of assumptions we make about female interaction in the workplace.

A study from the *Academy of Management Journal* asked people to read about conflict between two male co-workers, two female co-workers and one male and one female co-worker. The results found that conflict between two female co-workers was viewed as a problem far more than conflict between two male co-workers or a man and a woman. The women were seen as far more likely to quit as a result. (I can only imagine that the study's participants assumed that the women were plotting each other's deaths with a letter-opener while the men were simply 'hashing out some ideas' and 'letting off steam'.) Similarly, a 2009 poll carried out by OnePoll revealed that men gossip more in the office than women – an average of seventy-six minutes per day, compared with fifty-two for women – yet the myth still remains that this is a uniquely female trait.

But if every conflict between two women is a cat fight that must be picked over for days, and if every time you haul your team over the coals for messing up, you're a Queen Bee, trying to hold other women back, how is anyone ever meant to get anything done? As much as I prefer to avoid confrontation when I can, sometimes it happens, and sometimes it's even necessary. And some people, male or female, absolutely thrive on that sort of conflict. The frustration if you're an Alpha woman who finds herself stymied far more often than her male colleagues must be immense.

'I'm quite direct and tend to ask for exactly what I want without couching it in niceties,' explains Jackie, in her twenties, who works in advertising, and has been reprimanded at work for being too 'direct' with colleagues and clients. 'When I first started work, straight from university, I thought that was just what you did, and I think to an extent people were impressed with how assertive I was. It was only after a year or so, when I had my twelve-month review, that I found out how many people had complained about me being rude, or aggressive. There was no way that was my intention, I just didn't bother trying to qualify everything I said, or make every request sound like a question.'

She says she's softened herself a bit now, just because it's easier, but that it doesn't always sit comfortably with her. 'If I'm asking someone to do something, and it's part of their job, why do I have to make it sound like they're doing me a massive favour?'

I've worked with plenty of direct women, and I quite like it. As I've said, one of the reasons I've always enjoyed working for and with women is that I can normally work out where each one is coming from – even when I don't agree with her. I can normally work out what motivates her, why she's made the decision she has. But knowing what makes someone tick, and responding in a logical, non-emotional and fearless way, are two different things. And being a Beta to an Alpha boss can certainly have its pitfalls. How do you get your point across, and your own way on something you feel strongly about, when your superior's natural inclination is to pursue their own agenda rather than stop and consider yours?

'The risk is that you comply rather than hold your ground,' explains Eddie Erlandson. 'You hold your ground, you summarise, you state your view, rather than going into compliance and then resentment. So the risk of being a non-Alpha with an Alpha manager is that you end up wasting some of your great psychic energy in resentment and frustration and feeling controlled.'

The word 'control' is quite interesting. I used to work with a woman called Leanne, a senior female manager who was pretty Alpha, and was also very good at her job – very knowledgeable. A male colleague, who was junior to Leanne, was underperforming, and she got involved in trying to improve his performance. She was also one of the few people in the business who knew as much about his specialist subject as he did, if not more.

He totally refused to engage with her, resisted any attempts she made to manage him. And when he was asked, by a senior (male) colleague what he was playing at – he was in danger of losing his job – his response was, 'I don't like being controlled.'

I'm convinced he wouldn't have felt 'controlled' by a male colleague, he would have felt he was being 'managed'. But Alpha men are labelled 'decisive' where Alpha women are 'controlling' – like your nagging wife, or your mother-in-law.

And let's be clear. Assuming your boss isn't a tyrant or a bully, and assuming you're able to stand up for yourself when required, being a Beta sidekick to an Alpha boss can be wonderful and inspiring. The best kind of Alpha boss will bring out the best in you, will stop you quitting because something is hard, and will inject passion and energy into the most mundane project. When I talk to some of the Alpha women I know about their workloads and general life loads, I feel exhausted on their behalf, but they never look or sound it.

What about the dynamic in your friendship circle? When you think of all the Alpha women you know outside the workplace (and I believe that someone who's particularly Beta at work can still be very Alpha in their personal life and vice versa), they're the ones remembering to book tickets to the amazing exhibition that's opened, or the only person in your friendship group who will organise a villa for twenty people and dozens of budget airline flights so you all get to go on an amazing holiday together (she's already booked you into the best restaurant in town for your last night, bonus). In our personal lives, we need the Alphas: they're the doers, the make-things-happen guys, the leaders of men (women). And, in the same way, working for and with Alpha women can be crucial in injecting that all-important motivation and energy into our professional lives when we need it most.

They can be difficult, stubborn and sometimes pig-headed, sure. But they can also be insanely creative because their uncompromising worldview can create a truly original way of thinking. They care about their work, their people and their lives and, if you're lucky, a bit of that magic dust may rub off on you.

So never be put off a job because you've heard your new boss will be difficult, or high maintenance, or exacting. If you've also heard that they're great at what they do, that they inspire incredible loyalty in their team, if they're respected by everyone they know, then, chances are, it'll be totally worth it. You've just got to understand what motivates her, be honest about what motivates you, understand the parts you play and give it your all.

12.

BEING BATMAN WHEN YOU FEEL LIKE ROBIN
INSIDE: HOW TO DEAL WITH YOUR ALPHA TEAM
WHEN YOU'RE THE BETA BOSS

Despite spending most of my career trying to avoid being put in charge of everything, I've ended up as the boss several times, with varying degrees of success. Weirdly, I think it's because I'm such a classic Beta – it means I'm an excellent deputy: competent, confident and focused. So when the main role comes up, people naturally assume I'll be just as good stepping up. And I can do it. But it's been hard work getting there.

Being in charge has certainly never come naturally. I've had to feel my way around the role of boss, test my limits, work out how to make it fit me. And for great swathes of time, it's made me feel ill at ease. I certainly don't sit in the captain's seat, shift around a bit, think, This is nice, and start planning how to redecorate the office (this is a metaphor: obviously no one has an office of their own any more).

When I was younger it worked out fine because I ended up in charge of people I was already friends with. We had a decent enough personal relationship, and they were good enough at their jobs that everything just sort of worked out – although I suspect they didn't always love having an apparent 'boss' who turned to them for advice far more often than she dished it out.

Then there have been the occasions when it hasn't

worked. *At all*. I've found myself playing the role of subordinate to someone who sat below me on the team organogram. I've shied away from dealing with bad behaviour on my team until small issues have become massive problems, and there have been plenty of occasions when I've lacked the authority I needed. As a general rule, I'd always be fine if there was a big issue or crisis to deal with there and then. One quick burst of energy, knowing exactly what was needed, and I could deliver. But the minute the crisis was over, I'd lapse into my usual Beta self.

I don't do this too much any more – mainly because I've reached the point at work where I'm older and more experienced than my team. It means I have a certain level of authority that I can't shake off, no matter how many times I catch my shoelaces in the wheel of my chair and have to be rescued by the intern.

Kerry is thirty-eight and works in the media. Her early career was spent in all-male teams, and she would characterise as Alpha at work. She's now on a female-heavy team, under a woman she feels is extremely Beta – and it's not without its challenges. 'My boss is super-empathetic,' she explains. 'So gentle, really sweet and kind, but also incredibly passive-aggressive.

'If I do something wrong, or not the way she likes things done, she'll always say, "Don't worry, I probably didn't explain properly, or I may not even have told you," even though we both know she has. She can never just be straight and say, "Kerry, can you perhaps do it this way?" She dithers, and there always seems to be a worry about causing offence.'

I'm wary of conflating negative leadership traits with

being Beta, but I also recognise some of this in my own behaviour – apologising when you're asking for stuff to be done, for example. But Kerry, who's straightforward and straight-talking, just wants to be told when she's done something wrong. So her boss's behaviour leaves her feeling frustrated.

Another, very Alpha, woman I spoke to mentioned how frustrating she found her boss's desire to avoid confrontation. 'I see confrontation as part of communication and relationship building. They see it as scary and aggressive. But without that, how am I ever going to understand their point of view?'

I'm still very much a Beta, but the difference now is that I don't let my Beta traits morph into something more sinister. I embrace the Beta characteristics that make me good at my job, and I keep an eye on the ones that are less helpful. For example, I can be indecisive when I panic about doing the right thing and don't have all the information. So I've had to get better at asking more questions, and demanding more information from other people. In the past, I'd have panicked and put off making the decision until it had become a crisis that needed to be managed.

But when I look back to when I've been at my most Toxically Beta (indecisive, low energy, consumed by Impostor Syndrome), it strikes me that these were points when I was least happy and focused at work for a whole raft of reasons, very few of them to do with the job. I was emotionally overextended and it had a massive impact on my ability to manage a team or do my job.

I now know that my mind is on my job, and I have the time and the headspace to make thoughtful decisions

I'm happy to stand by, and be strategic so I know I'm not wasting my energy in the wrong places. Then everything tends to fall into place. Being busy is fine – in fact, it's preferable to the alternative – but it has to be my decision.

On the other hand, the minute my back is against the wall or I'm playing catch-up to everyone else, or I'm being pressured into doing things I don't think I've got the time, information or knowledge to make an informed decision about, I revert back to the most Beta version of myself possible.

And that's why having Alpha team members can unnerve me more than having an Alpha boss. When you have a passionate, hard-working, talented Alpha woman working for you, they want to move things on, make things better, keep pushing everything, which is great. But they want to do it at their pace. And their pace might not be right for me. Instead of telling them to slow down and taking control of the situation, I tend to shut down, frustrating myself, and frustrating them even more.

Which is a problem that spirals into lunacy if you're like me, and your natural instinct is to give your team what you think they want above what you want. The danger is you end up negating what you need from them (which is why they're there in the first place). And, trust me, nothing can make you feel more Beta than the realisation that your entire focus is around meeting your team's needs, whims and timelines rather than your own.

So what's to be done?

You can fight it, try to be more Alpha than the Alphas, but that really isn't sustainable. Put all your energy into trying to be something you're not, and that's all your energy gone.

What if you don't have time on your side to gain authority over your team through age alone? What if you're younger and less experienced than some of your colleagues and need to fake authority? Or what if you're older and more experienced but they're just really, really Alpha?

How do you do it without compromising your sense of self and who you are? How do you find your inner bad-ass boss without becoming a shoulder-padded caricature of what you imagine she should be like?

Embrace your Beta to unlock your Alpha.

I suspect that none of us is quite as Beta (or, indeed, Alpha) as we think we are. I say this because we're all so complex: our emotions, experiences, reactions and triggers all vary wildly, yet we rarely consider the facets of our personalities, especially in the workplace, where everyone's behaviour is so loaded and layered with meaning. But imagine what would happen if we were able to unlock these dormant, hitherto undiscovered elements of our personality and deploy them as and when required, just to get the job done. It's not about changing who we are to fit in better, it's about making better use of the tool we already have at our disposal – our massive, amazing, brilliant brains.

For example, although I identify as Beta, and no one who knows me has ever really questioned that, I've always suspected that I may have a few dormant Alpha traits, which are far more likely to emerge when I'm confident, or fired up, or excited about a project.

I want to find out a bit more about myself and why I

respond as I do to different work situations. Tania Hummel, the executive coach and HR consultant, suggests I try a couple of psychometric tests by a company called Lumina, which she uses with her clients. 'They tell you what your strengths are, but also your weaknesses, outline areas of development for you and advise on how to deal with people who are different from you.' Which is exactly what I'm after. But the tests also look at and compare our natural self, our everyday self and the type of person we are when we're overextended, which means stressed out or over-whelmed. (Again, exactly what I'm after: I've always suspected that long periods of stress exacerbate my most negative Beta tendencies.)

I complete two tests, called Spark and Emotion, and each questionnaire takes fifteen to twenty minutes to do online. They're both multiple choice, asking me how I respond to certain scenarios, and how certain scenarios make me feel.

Lumina doesn't use words like Alpha and Beta to describe people: they prefer to refer to 'traits' rather than types. But when Tania looks at my profile, she immediately tells me I am 'people-focused, inspiration-driven, and big-picture thinking'. This is all stuff I know, but it's nice to have it confirmed. Tania also says that I have a lot of 'green' traits (traits are divided into four main groups, red, green, yellow and blue). I'm sure you can see where I'm going with this: green is the most Beta group of traits, red is the most Alpha. 'So you're hugely accommodating,' Tania explains. 'Hugely intimate, very empathetic, very adaptable. You're imaginative, sociable, conceptual.' And my least preferred traits? 'Tough, competitive, takes charge, purposeful, but still quite logical.' Ah.

Talking through all of this confirms that I'm as Beta as I thought I was. But how does the information help me deal with an Alpha team?

For starters, the tests explore how my behaviour or traits change when I get stressed or emotionally overextended. For example, they highlight that I'm a good listener in everyday life, but when I'm overextended I become more so and this becomes a negative trait. I become passive. Also, I have a strong collaborative streak that becomes more prominent when I'm overextended, at which point I become obsessed with everyone else's happiness beyond the task at hand.

These are both true, and tap into what I view as my negative Beta qualities. But by pinpointing exactly what they are, and when they occur, I can work on them specifically (by making a concerted effort to become more decisive and vocal when I'm under stress). I can be more effective without fundamentally changing who I am.

So if I can switch on more of my Alpha side when I need to, giving someone a stern telling-off or confronting them a difficult situation straight away becomes less of a slog.

I already know that I'm more Beta when I'm under pressure and when I have less time to make decisions (or when other people are pushing me to make decisions I haven't had a chance to get my head around), but I've also grasped that I become my most Beta self when I'm bored, or when I'm not interested in what's going on around me. And I've always struggled with that feeling of inertia and low energy when nothing exciting is going on.

I guess it's efficiency – if my brain doesn't feel the need to engage in what's going on around me then it just doesn't.

When I'm busy and focused, with deadlines, challenges and projects I'm interested in, my brain responds in kind. I'm high energy and efficient. I'm decisive and cut to the chase – I simply have to. In the immediate aftermath I continue to be efficient, organised and decisive until I reach a point where I don't have to any more. Then I get bored and I switch off.

Working this out was fantastic because it made me realise that Beta-ness isn't about me being lazy, or a pathological people-pleaser. It's about what motivates me.

For example, how I manage my day and my time is key. When I first started working in magazines, we had a monthly schedule we had to stick to like clockwork – we had a final deadline we were all working towards, which was characterised by late nights and an intense flurry of work. After that we were all working towards the next deadline. It suited me really well, but working on a website is a different kettle of fish. Our deadlines are hourly, not monthly, which can be very intense when you're not used to it, but becomes less of an event over time. And that's when I get bored.

So, once I cottoned on to how my time and energy levels were linked to my inherent Beta-ness, I changed things. I've started imposing hard deadlines on myself to get certain things done to ensure that I'm busier for the first four days of the week, then give myself Fridays for admin and implementation, so I don't burn out. Admin can become an endless, ever-expanding act of procrastination if I start the week with it, so forcing myself to crack on with the big stuff straight away means it actually gets done. If I find myself doing too many dull or routine jobs in one week, I make sure I have some harder or more engaging work to do too, just to keep my brain switched on.

All of this makes me a more engaged boss. It makes me more alert and decisive and means I tend to have more energy. In short, I've found out how to borrow a bit of Alpha without changing who I am or how I behave.

The thing with psychometric tests or personality tests, or those quizzes at the back of a magazine, is that they tell you a tiny bit more about yourself. They won't necessarily give you the vital piece of information that makes everything in your life fall into place, but they might offer a snippet of insight into why you do and say things in a certain way, and how you can change those things without compromising who you are. For me, it was about seeing my personality traits – negative and positive – as small parts of a bigger picture that can be controlled and tweaked by me as required, rather than a stick with which to beat myself up.

Beta women aren't fundamentally 'lazy' or 'pushovers' and Alpha women aren't essentially 'bitches' or 'control freaks': we're just motivated by different things.

And that's at the heart of any careers manual you'll read, including this one. It's about finding out who you are and what you need, then working out how to get what you need to be the version of yourself you want to be in the workplace. It's never about faking it or being someone you're not. It's about embracing your own traits and quirks, and reminding everyone else how wonderful they are.

13.

HOW TO DEAL WITH SEXISM IN THE WORKPLACE WHEN YOU'RE BETA, ALPHA OR JUST A WOMAN

I've never been confronted with the overt, inherent sexism you read about in the papers, where women are fired from their high-powered City jobs for refusing to get their tits out or get off with a lap dancer at their office summer party at Stringfellows (I'm paraphrasing, but you get the gist).

In fact, ask me at twenty-three, twenty-six or twenty-eight about examples of sexism I'd faced at work and I'd have struggled to come up with any. Because often (but not always) when you work in a female-dominated industry, like I do, sexism comes in subtler, more insidious forms, plenty of which have only been revealed to me as I've got older. Apart from anything else, if you've got your head down and are desperately trying to do your job without messing up anything too drastically (which basically defined my working life in my twenties), it's easy to miss what's going on around you. Also, as you get older you gain a bit of perspective on how other people work. Getting your backside grabbed by a much older male colleague in the pub isn't about sex it's about power. The guy you work with who makes a not-that-quiet comment about your breasts to his mates when you're getting a mug out of the dishwasher isn't trying to make them laugh: he's exerting his authority. Actually . . . maybe I've witnessed more sexism at work than I first thought.

It's only now that I see how often women get boxed in as 'easy-going' or a 'bitch' (potentially any woman who disagrees with the general male consensus).

I've definitely found myself in situations in my career where my opinion hasn't been sought on something I know more about than anyone else in the building. I've also overheard (male) colleagues agreeing to keep 'tricky' (argumentative, probably Alpha) women out of the loop because they didn't want them to 'complicate issues' round specific projects (the same projects that would later go tits up because no one was asking the right questions from the outset). One woman I know, who works for a male-dominated tech company (in a non-technical role) has been told that there's no point in her coming to meetings because the team 'will just be talking tech-speak the whole time, so I won't understand it'. She was then told it was actually because her habit of asking difficult questions was 'making the project lose focus'.

The result is that in some of the (fairly evenly gendered) offices I've worked in everything seemed to descend into boys' and girls' clubs with men disappearing for secret meetings that female team members were either too unimportant or too 'difficult' to consult on, while said women huddled together to complain about all the projects they were being phased out of.

It's not the case everywhere I've worked, but the formation of boys' clubs, even in an industry as dominated by women as mine, doesn't seem to be anything new or surprising. I canvassed Alpha and Beta friends in similar jobs to mine, and they've all seen similar things.

The only way around it? 'Be the *über*-bitch,' suggests

a former colleague, who, although quite Alpha by my standards, is in awe of her high Alpha boss, who gets her own way (and sets her own agenda) by making it clear, in no uncertain terms, that she's the Alpha in any room she walks into – whatever the room's gender mix. 'She [her boss] screams so loud and makes such a fuss that she always gets what she wants done,' my friend explains. 'It must be exhausting being like that all the time, though.'

But when you're a Beta woman, like me, when you aren't naturally loud, pushy or outspoken, how do you navigate sexism in the workplace when it exists to keep you quiet, keep you small, and keep you in your place?

Christine, thirty, works in the property industry. Her experience at her first job reads like the sort of cautionary tale HR executives would share on a training day. It ticks virtually every imaginable box for sexism in the workplace. A full house in the game of sexual-harassment bingo, if you will.

'It was an all-male team,' she tells me. 'I was one of only two women there. The entire team were straight white men, with the exception of one gay man.

'Over the four years I was there, my boss would constantly share his theories on male/female dynamics, his favourite being the "thirty power switch" – the idea that when women reach thirty they lose all their sexual power and men gain it, and therefore want to date twenty-two-year-olds. I was repeatedly told that I didn't need a pay rise because I would just get married and my future husband would give me money. I was repeatedly told, "I can't wait until you come in here and tell me you need nine months off because you're going to have a baby. Women are all the same." I was twenty-two and single.

'Oh, and he would call me into his office for some spurious reason, then tell me to hang on because he had to reply to an email – he didn't realise that I could see the reflection of his computer in the window behind him. He was watching porn every time.'

Christine stuck it out because she needed the work, and left as soon as she got a better job offer. But in an all-male company where this culture was rife, she simply didn't believe there was any way she could speak out. And as much as I'd love the story to end with Christine righteously taking her old boss down (he was eventually fired for a series of other misdemeanours when he sufficiently creeped-out a more senior female member of staff and HR started digging around), I would never suggest that she should have been the one to stick her neck out and make a fuss. And, frankly, I have no idea what I would have done differently in that scenario.

The problem is, it's tough to give advice on how to deal with sexism, or even sexual harassment, in the workplace without putting the onus on women to sort it out. When someone develops coping mechanisms in the workplace to get their voice heard, or just to get through the day, they might not be that helpful to the wider workplace culture, but sometimes just getting to the end of the day, or getting that project out of the door, is all you can think of, and that's okay.

'I've totally done it,' admits my friend Rachel, who's in her late thirties and works for the HR department of a bank in the City. 'I've let gross comments slide, because

I'd spend my life in confrontation with people otherwise. On the other hand, it's not a great example to set to anyone. I'm fully aware that if I don't do something about it it'll never stop, but it's also exhausting and only ever seems to make my working day harder.'

Equally, if you quit a working environment because the casual sexism, outright misogyny or full-on sexual harassment is too much to deal with, should you feel guilty about letting down the sisterhood? Of course not. But we all internalise these things, make them about ourselves and our behaviour, when really they're about the system we're living in.

If your boss is sexist, it's because he's a sexist person, not because you don't know how to charm him. He is in the wrong, not you. If one of your male colleagues speaks over you in a meeting, takes your suggestion as his own, and everyone else lets him have the credit, the culture of your workplace needs serious work. But is it your fault for not screaming him down in public until he conceded that it was originally your idea? Of course not. Very few people would feel comfortable demonstrating that sort of behaviour in the workplace and you shouldn't have to do so because one of your colleagues can't be trusted to act courteously and professionally.

If you're being sexually harassed at work, or if you've been sexually assaulted by one of your colleagues, it doesn't matter what you wore. It doesn't matter how many drinks you had in the pub after work. It doesn't matter if you were the only person who laughed at their bad jokes. Not only were they in the wrong, they were also breaking the law. You weren't responsible for any one of those tiny decisions they made in the run-up to their one big decision to feel you up in the smoking area at the back of the office, or take you back to theirs for sex after the work Christmas party when you were semi-conscious.

I have to say that now, explicitly and clearly, because we (women) are very good at blaming ourselves for behaviour that isn't our fault. We internalise the sexism we're faced with. We allow someone to write off sexual harassment as 'a bit of fun' because we feel inexplicably guilty about it when someone else has committed an actual crime against us.

Whether it's thinking we need to be the last in the bar at night and the first up for breakfast the next day at a conference filled with male colleagues, or laughing off office banter that's (a) not funny, and (b) an HR nightmare in the making, for fear of getting a reputation for being a misery, we become adept at moulding ourselves to fit the environment we're in – even if that environment is hostile. It's a great life skill when you're shipwrecked on a deserted island, but knackering the rest of the time.

And that's why any advice I give you here on how to get through the day is just advice on how to get through the day, how to get that project out of the door and how to achieve the things at work that are actually important to you. I'd love to tell you these things will smash the patriarchy and change the world, but if I knew how to do that, this would be a very different book.

However, every time I find myself laughing at a faintly gross joke in the office because I 'don't want to cause a fuss' or 'be *that* person' (full disclosure: I've done it lots, and I've done it recently), I think about a woman I used to work with. She was really great at her job and made a massive impact on the brand she worked on. The (all-male) tech team had a couple of running jokes about her. Nothing major or particularly cruel in the grand scheme of things (and, honestly, these were pretty nice blokes for the most part). It was a couple of little cues that one of them would pick up whenever her name was mentioned, causing the others to snigger and join in. Childish stuff, and she may have known about it. I'm not convinced she'd have cared either way. But why did they do it?

Because they were, collectively, a lazy, apathetic and poorly run team. They weren't untalented, but getting them to inject a bit of drive or passion into a project was almost impossible. And she was the only person who called them out on it. She'd go down there and demand a response. She'd tell them off when stuff wasn't delivered on time and, in no uncertain terms, when their work wasn't good enough.

Basically, she showed them up, and rather than considering that there might be something in it, they took the piss, just a little, just among themselves, to undermine her. Because she was very, very good at her job, and they just weren't as good at theirs.

So now every time I worry about being the butt of a male team's jokes or dubbed 'the boring one', 'the shouty one' or, *eye-roll*, 'the feminist one', I remember her, how good she was at her job, and resolve to be more like her, and less like them.

The problem I've always had is that most of the advice knocking around on how to deal with men in the workplace always seems to revolve around beating them at their own game (earlier Eddie Erlandson described how his wife adopted specific physical traits, leaning forward, banging her hand on the table, to deal with her Alpha male colleagues). An Alpha woman could do this but a Beta?

I used to work with Sian, who was, by her own admission, an Alpha with Beta tendencies. She could be very chilled out and easy-going, yet she was also capable of switching on the Alpha when required. And I only saw her do so with one guy. In meetings he would constantly talk over her, cut her off, interrupt and misinterpret what she was trying to say. 'The stupid thing is, he was my friend,' she told me recently, when I asked her about those meetings. 'I go round to his house, I hang out with him and his wife, but in those work scenarios, he was a total nightmare.'

Her response was to confront it head on: she told him, in no uncertain terms, to stop interrupting her, and she did it every time until he gave in. But you've got to have guts to do that. I'm sure my response would have been just to stop talking in those meetings.

So what do you do?

I've only ever worked on an all-male team once, for a relatively short period. I enjoyed it for lots of reasons – it was fun, social, and everyone was clever and creative. But it was also far more testosterone-fuelled than anything I've experienced before or since. The veneer of politeness that characterises so many of our interactions in the workplace just wasn't there – and without it I floundered.

If someone thought a piece of work was rubbish, they'd loudly ask, 'Who did this shit?' and whoever had produced it would say, 'That was me – what's wrong with it?' And they'd have a bit of a shout, then eventually reach some sort of consensus on what needed to be done to improve it. Then everyone went back to work, no one took offence, and it was never mentioned again. There was no negative atmosphere; nothing was ever left to fester. All great.

Except when I was the culprit. Then, when someone shouted, 'Who wrote this feature? It's total crap,' I'd sit silently, wide-eyed and pale, staring at my screen, totally at a loss as to how to respond. Eventually I'd put my hand up and whisper, 'It was me . . . but what's wrong with it? I thought it was okay.' I sounded whiny and unsure, and I certainly wasn't taking the opportunity to robustly defend my work. Because if someone else is kicking off, my default position is to shut down. I can't help it, it's instinctive, and I'm certainly not the only one who does it.

And if I don't like environments where people are talking over me, you can imagine how I felt in meetings when everyone was yelling at each other – which happened a lot. I should probably have adopted a 'when in Rome' approach and joined in. But for all my desire to dial up my latent Alpha, that sort of direct confrontation fills me with fear and dread. And it also comes back to style over substance: slamming your hand on the desk and shouting is all well and good when you've got an important point to make, but if you're arguing over the exact wording of a picture caption? Is it worth it? Shouting for the sake of shouting, fighting for no discernible purpose, seems pointless to me – which is probably what marks me out as Beta.

But that's why I like a working environment in which everyone is polite to each other. Yes, politeness can sometimes mean you don't get your point across. And, yes, there is a fine line between pursed-lipped politeness and passive-aggression, which we've all crossed, but I'd take that over an environment in which everyone's constantly shouting about how terrible everyone else is at their job.

And for all the talk about female-only environments being hotbeds of bitchiness and simmering resentment, almost all the women I have worked with have been huge champions of each other's work, loudly praising each other when they've done something brilliantly, talking openly and admiringly about women whose work they love. Maybe I've been lucky, but anyone who says you can't have a creative, dynamic, positive environment without the shouting is just plain wrong.

The other thing I found tricky was the bantz, the constant piss-taking. In normal, day-to-day life, I'm relatively thick skinned – probably more so than some of the blokes I was working with. But I can only presume that they have a banter switch somewhere in their brains that I don't know about, allowing them to absorb every lolz that was chucked their way, process whether or not they could be bothered to take offence, then lob something just as 'hilarious' back. I found it exhausting. It meant I could never relax, or just focus on the task at hand. A bit of my brain constantly had to be focused elsewhere on the Top Chat, which was basically verbal willy-waving, to make sure I didn't miss the joke or become the butt of it.

Although admittedly the time I snuck in early and moved the keys about on everyone's keyboards was pretty funny.

Maybe once you've stripped out the overt sexism, the sexual harassment, the gender pay gap, all the big, loud stuff that we know is Really Bad and needs dealing with, working in an environment that's overtly and specifically geared towards men comes down to one thing for me: it's exhausting. It's exhausting having to pretend. Having to try to fit into something that's just wrong for you. (I certainly can't speak for everyone here – maybe you work in an all-male environment and love it.)

Remember, the working world is set up for men to succeed in: we're still interlopers, and we're not allowed to forget it.

Whether you're Alpha or Beta, negotiating a workplace that's inherently male, as so many are, is so hard because most workplaces – and the very institution of work – are not designed for women's progress or comfort. They've evolved over history with a very different purpose in mind. We talk about the big stuff all the time because it's newsworthy, it's noteworthy. But the daily grind of just finding a way to fit in, not falling off the banter bus, not being so po-faced that you stop being a laugh, that's not noteworthy: that's just life.

SEXISM AT WORK

Being mistaken for the secretary; being asked to take notes in a meeting, even though you've already explained that you're not the secretary; being asked when you're planning to have children in a job interview, even though that's totally illegal; being asked to fetch drinks for a meeting even though you're the third most senior person in the room; being expected to order the team's stationery even though you're the second most senior person on the team and the

214

busiest. These are all punchlines to a bad joke about sexism in the office and all happen to actual women every day.

And the sliding scale from a bit creepy to sexual harassment gets blurred with paternalism and ownership. I questioned a lot of women about their experiences of dealing with male bosses and male teams, without specifically asking them about sexual harassment or assault. And that's when the in-between stories emerged. The ones women didn't necessarily want to describe as sexual harassment, because what had happened didn't seem to go far enough. The stories of male bosses who were too married, too proper or too scared of getting caught to sexually harass a female member of their team but felt they had a proprietary relationship, nonetheless.

One woman I spoke to, who worked in a very male-dominated industry, found her older male boss particularly tricky to negotiate. 'He insisted on a very close relationship. He needed to know everything about what I was doing, including my personal life, and he took offence when I started dating someone at work – but only because I hadn't asked his permission first! Even though I was under no obligation to do so. He also took offence when I became more confident working for another boss.'

Another woman told me how, when she was just starting out in tech, she took on some contract work for a guy who promised to 'show her the ropes'. The role turned out to be that of a glorified PA. A few weeks in, they were scouting venues for an event. In one restaurant he burst into tears and said he was getting a divorce. 'I've always known, don't go anywhere near the guy who starts saying that his wife doesn't understand him,' she told me. 'I was really young, but even then, there was no way I was falling for that. So I picked up some serviettes from the side, gave them to him and left the venue.'

She was confident she'd done the right thing, the smart thing. A few days later, he told her that the project was over and her services were no longer required.

SEXUAL HARASSMENT AND SEXUAL ASSAULT

The big stuff is unfortunately all too common. A 2016 TUC study found that 52 per cent of women have experienced sexual harassment at work – this goes up to 63 per cent of women aged between eighteen and twenty-four. The debate around whether women could or should be more Alpha or Beta in the workplace carries little worth when you consider that it doesn't matter what personality type you are, how you do your job, or the role you have, at least half of all women will face sexual harassment or assault just for doing their job. It has nothing to do with women's behaviour or performance at work, but it is a reality many have to negotiate every day.

Sexual harassment and assault in the workplace are a power play. They're a short hop, skip and a jump from the 'joke' comment about your ovaries in that board meeting, which was your colleague's way of reminding everyone else in the room that you had no right to be there. It's a sliding scale from the bloke who whispers 'I would' to your boss as you bend over to try to fix the printer (because none of them is even attempting it) and the guy who thinks it's okay to grab your breasts when you're alone in a meeting room because 'they're there'. And it's not about your breasts or your ovaries. It's about reminding you who's in control, whose house you're in and who's the interloper.

If you want to know just how sinister those power plays can be, we should return to Christine. When she was explaining why she didn't report her old boss, she said a bit more about the complexities of their relationship. 'It was my first job so I didn't realise how abnormal it was. And he'd always tell me how HR wasn't my friend and how I should never report anything to them because they'd always report it back to the person you were complaining about.

'I grew up with abusive parents, and had abusive partners from the age of sixteen. My boss told me this was what the workplace was like, and I believed him. He cried when I left, and we stayed in touch for a bit afterwards – it was only once I'd been away for a few months that I realised how weird the whole thing had been.'

I could give you some tips on how to deal with being sexually harassed or sexually assaulted in the workplace, but I won't because there are so many variables at play there. Not everyone can stand up for themselves in the workplace, or has someone to do it for them. Maybe the fear of being fired and the need to pay your rent is too real. Maybe your boss, the HR director or the chief executive was the person who attacked you. Maybe you just cannot bring yourself to talk about it. But if you're working somewhere you really feel you won't be backed up, believed and supported, then you have to make it your priority to remove yourself from that environment. Leaving doesn't make you weak, or a failure, and it certainly doesn't make it your fault.

And obviously if you can, report it, shout it from the rooftops, make it a problem for the person who attacked you – make it a problem for your boss, the head of HR or the chief executive. Make it anyone's problem but yours to deal with.

To an extent Alpha or Beta doesn't really matter when it comes down to stuff like this. Stuff that reminds us how relatively recent women's mainstream acceptance in the workplace is, and how tenuous our place at the table as equals. Many women won't be sexually harassed or assaulted at work, but plenty will. Too many. Most women, though, will have to find coping tools to deal with sexism in the workplace – whether it's overt or insidious. Acts of sexism chip away at our right to be there at all.

And let's not forget that sexism in all its guises is designed to shut us up. Anyone trying to shut me up at the earliest points in my career would have had a devastating impact on my later success. As a Beta woman, I've needed to be coaxed into making my voice heard, and twenty-two-year-old me would have become quieter, smaller, less significant, with a boss like Christine's. And maybe that's why, in many industries, only the women who shout the loudest make it to the top. Because, as it stands, that's the only way to front down the breast-grabbers, the banter machines and the office chair sexists. By being more Alpha. And that has to change.

But it's not all bad and it's not hopeless. We don't need to shut up and put up with it, but we do need to do our bit to be bigger and louder wherever we can, so we can make things better for the women who can't make a noise or kick up a fuss.

All of us – Alpha, Beta, women or men – need to change the shape of the table so that it's the right fit for everyone. So that it doesn't turn half its occupants into victims.

14.

ALPHA OR BETA, IS ONE EVER BETTER THAN THE OTHER?

So the big question is here. Alpha or Beta women: which is better? Only kidding – I'm not here to pit women against each other. We have the internet, popular culture and certain sections of the media to do that for us.

Because, actually, it doesn't matter whether we're Alpha or Beta – they're just new ways to put us in a box and keep us in our place. What does matter is that we get to understand who we are and how we tick and be that person in the workplace without being told we're 'unprofessional', 'too aggressive' or 'overly emotional' (or whatever particular crime you or I have committed against the Gods of Office Politics this time).

And that in itself is why there's never been a more important time to discuss these issues. One of the words used to describe Alpha women in a derogatory way is 'nasty' – Alpha women are bossy, bitchy, controlling and nasty.

Nasty Woman was famously co-opted by women all over the world after Donald Trump referred to Hillary Clinton as such during the 2016 presidential election debates. He claimed she was 'such a nasty woman' when she made a dig at him during the debate over Medicare (this from the man who had repeatedly attacked her during the campaign, leading chants to 'lock her up' at his rallies).

By calling her 'nasty', he was attempting to denigrate her, to dismiss what she was saying as the words of a bitchy woman with an axe to grind. Instead it became a rallying cry for women who were willing to stand up and be counted to have their say and to stand up for what they believed in, in a world where being a woman who's too loud, too opinionated, too much is harder than ever.

Equally, it's as important for me to know, as a Beta woman, how I can turn my natural strengths into personally fulfilling and successful career opportunities, without wasting my time and energy trying to be something I'm not, as it is for an Alpha woman to find out how she can harness her drive and passion and turn it into something that showcases her talents and means she's not constantly banging her head against a brick wall.

Because OF COURSE you can be a good leader if you aren't Alpha. It's about what you do, not who you are. Believing that we can't is holding us back. And substitute 'Alpha' for 'masculine' and what do you get? Forty-seven per cent of the workforce believing that to succeed they need to change who they are and how they work.

It matters, because our whole attitude to work can shift on it. Believing that I wasn't 'the right sort of editor' held me back. It took me a decade to realise that even though I had none of the obvious personality traits that I imagined were needed in my role, I'm good at my job. But, really, I became a good editor when I stopped questioning whether I was the right person to do the job and started focusing on my strengths – which, incidentally, are all Beta traits. I'm collaborative, good with people, happy to get my hands dirty and work hard. I also faced my Beta weaknesses and considered how to be more Alpha in those areas.

What I realised, in the end, is that no one is all good

or all bad at their job: we all have strengths and weak-nesses. And I may sound like Captain Obvious, but that gets lost in all the noise, the endless posturing and constant comparisons we make with each other. And even if it is obvious, I only got there in the most roundabout way, and perhaps never would have done so at all if I hadn't started examining properly who I was and how I worked.

The idea for *Beta* came about after I wrote an article about being a Beta boss with an Alpha team. It started off as a lament, because I felt you couldn't do it and I couldn't do it. But speaking to careers experts and psychologists when I was researching the piece forced me to think about what I was good at for the first time in ages. It also offered me a bit of perspective on the things I wasn't so great at: they weren't that bad, they weren't deal-breakers, and they were things that I could probably work on, if I was willing to embrace them head on rather than shy away from them. It also reminded me – sharply – that I'd spent all this time worrying about how bad I was at my job, panicking, making myself and the role smaller than they could be, and all the while I was doing the job, and doing it well. I was succeeding – but I worried so much that my personality didn't fit that I barely noticed.

The difference was almost instantaneous. Suddenly I looked forward to going into work every day. Sunday-night fear was almost eradicated, and challenges became something to embrace. I remembered that I loved my job, and I cared about it, and that I needed to nurture it more, rather than treating it like an unexploded bomb that might go off at any moment. I stopped treating work as something to be fearful of lest the bomb exploded and everyone saw me for a fraud who should never have been given the job in the first place.

The amount of headspace my own personal brand of Impostor Syndrome must have taken up was incredible: suddenly I could engage my brain again. I had time to think, consider things, take a decision without freaking out that it was going to be the wrong one. I'm not constantly exhausted (feeling like you're wearing the wrong boots all the time is exhausting), which means I can take on more, be more dynamic and passionate. I can be a bit more Alpha when I want or need to be.

If this all sounds a bit too vague, here are some of the things I have always dismissed as 'not the sort of thing I do' that I now do. Not because I'm always great at them but because my fear of doing them wrongly doesn't paralyse me any more.

PUBLIC SPEAKING

I'm still terrified of this one, but I make a point of doing it every time I'm asked. Sometimes it goes well, sometimes not, but I'm trying to train myself to see the occasions where it goes badly as progress in their own way. (Full disclosure: last time I had to speak in front of twenty people I had to lock myself into a toilet cubicle for half an hour afterwards to calm myself down. I'm really not as chilled out and Zen as I'm making it sound.)

RADIO OR TV

See above. I get massive tunnel vision about thirty seconds beforehand, but I'll always take the opportunity if I get it. And I have even been known to enjoy myself.

I always told myself that my talent was in enabling other people to do a great job, and that, although I could be creative, I wasn't the sort of person who could generate lots of good ideas. I also told myself I wasn't commercial, wasn't good in front of clients. I told myself that I was good at the housekeeping stuff – keeping everything ticking over, making sure everyone else was happy. It's all hard work, but it's not difficult – it's also sometimes thankless and dull. But that's who I thought I was, the safe pair of hands who wouldn't do anything stupid, but certainly not someone with huge amounts of creative flair or enough charisma to sell an idea.

Once I learnt to relax and embrace my strengths, I remembered that, actually, I'm good with ideas. I'm creative and I'm good with people. In fact, those were some of the reasons why I became a journalist, and why I was given my job. But I got so used to trying to keep my head down, not make too many big mistakes, not draw too much attention to myself, that I went for the lowest risk strategy possible. I became dull but reliable at my job, when what was really needed was someone who wasn't scared of making a mistake occasionally.

None of these things changed because I changed as a person, but because I stopped thinking I needed to change as a person.

So why is this a women's problem, not a people's problem? To an extent, I'm sure, it is also a problem for men, but then again, almost every single woman I spoke to said she had suffered from Impostor Syndrome in her career, and I've never come across a man who feels that way. (There's no real consensus on whether this is more of a female issue:

some studies suggest that men and women get Impostor Syndrome in equal measure, others that men are less affected by it as they are raised to bluff and exaggerate.)

One woman I spoke to told me that her old boss used to turn down her requests for pay rises (while awarding them to male members of the team) because 'she was lucky to be there in the first place'. That he felt he could say that out loud demonstrates just what a dinosaur he was, but workplace sexism is still depressingly rife – and Impostor Syndrome still depressingly potent – because plenty of people are still thinking it. And while some people still believe women are lucky to be allowed to participate in the workplace at all, women will only succeed by shouting the loudest, by being the most Alpha of the Alpha. And the rest of us? We will become smaller, quieter and less significant. Not because we can't succeed, but because the world doesn't want to make room for us.

So what do we do? How do we change the script, and the accepted expectations for what a successful woman looks like? I can't tell you what will change the world, and I can't tell you what to do, but I can tell you what worked for me, and I can tell you what I wished I'd known when I was twenty-one.

1. WORK OUT WHAT MOTIVATES YOU

I'm serious. Before you start worrying about what your boss and your company want, think about what *you* want, and why you're there. No one loves their job all day every day. But even if you clock in for eight hours a day just to fund your secret passion for making terrariums, that's still eight hours a day, five days a week. It's a long time to spend doing something that doesn't motivate you in any way. Whether it's the satisfaction you get from completing a task, the colleague who has become a best friend, or even being able to go for a pint on a Friday night and feeling like you've earned it, work out what presses your buttons and how you can do more of the same. Any opportunity you get to make your job more fun or engaging, take it. Work won't always be fun, but it doesn't necessarily have to be miserable either.

2. YOUR JOB SHOULD WORK FOR YOU AS MUCH AS YOU WORK FOR IT

Is your job giving you the opportunities you were told about when you interviewed for it? Do you still get to travel as much as you'd like? Are you being given new challenges? Are you being properly compensated for the work you do? We all get stuck in work ruts, and I always feel like they happen to me more when I feel I have no choice other than to turn up each day and get on with the grind, no escape plan. But, actually, we do have options and we do have power. If you want more out of your job, say so. Fight for it. There's a reason why you took that job, and you sometimes need to remind yourself of what it is. And if that reason no longer applies, or your boss can't or won't give you what you want, then it's time to look elsewhere.

3. DON'T TURN DOWN THE HARD STUFF

Take on the challenges, and embrace them. Finding them difficult, and not getting things right first time, doesn't

mean you've failed: it means you're working stuff o_
try to alternate every three or six months now – I p_
myself, try new stuff, do things that are hard, then ea_
off for a while. I actually learn from it, and am not jus_
in a constant state of panic or stress when I'm continuously
out of my comfort zone and never have time to think about
what I'm doing or why.

4. REMEMBER THAT THE WORST-CASE SCENARIO IS NEVER THAT BAD

What's your worst-case scenario at work? Mine is always
being fired in a way that results in public shaming within
my industry. People would *know*, I'd think. They'd *talk*
about it.

And, yes, were I to be fired publicly from my job (which
seems unlikely), I'm sure it would garner a bit of gossip.
But that would be it. Nothing bad would happen, really.
People would forget about it eventually. And being the topic
of gossip isn't necessarily that bad – most people are too
polite to come up and talk to you about your very public
firing. Unless you do an important job – you're a police
officer or a doctor, for instance – then the worst-case
scenario is rarely that bad.

5. DON'T ASSUME EVERYONE ELSE IS BEING POLITE – IF YOU'RE DOING A POOR JOB, SOMEONE *WILL* TELL YOU

This is crucial. Is your boss an idiot? Okay, maybe, but is
their boss an idiot? Or their boss? At least one person you
work for will have their head screwed on, and they won't

aying you to come in every day and do a bad job. No is that nice. If you're messing stuff up, someone will 1 you. If you're constantly messing things up, they will ave a slightly more formal word with you about it. If you absolutely cannot do anything right, well, yes, you might get fired, but by that time you'll know all about it. People won't pay you to be bad at your job. They won't spare your blushes and let you mess up over and over again just because they feel sorry for you. And you did not get that promotion because you once complimented your boss's tie: you got it because you earned it. You deserve your job and you're great at it. If that wasn't true you just wouldn't be there.

6. BUT ONE LAST THING . . .

Not everyone is great at their job all day every day. We all have off days, or afternoons when we just can't concentrate, or make a decision, or get something off the ground as quickly as we'd like. If that happens once a week, and it's usually on a Wednesday after you had a jacket potato at lunch, well, put it down to a Hump-day carb overload and don't worry about it too much. Do your expenses, sort out your email inbox and put that big creative project off until tomorrow. Everyone does it, even the people who are pretending otherwise on Instagram.

But if you feel like that most days, or most afternoons, then you need to think about that too. Because you shouldn't. Are you depressed? Unmotivated? Knackered? Bored? Because you can do something about all of those things. It doesn't mean you're lazy or useless. It just means

something isn't connecting right now. So stop beati...
self up, take a deep breath and reset.

But mainly what I wish I'd been told at twenty-one is t...
you have to work at your job if you want it to make y...
happy. You have to give it time and love in the same way
as you have to give a relationship some love if you want it
to work. But in the same way as a relationship should give
you more than it takes, your job shouldn't suck out your
soul. It should give you more than it takes. Because you're
great and you deserve to spend forty hours a week doing
something you like, in a way that feels true to you.

If you can give yourself the opportunity and the headspace
to focus on the job at hand, and what you bring to the table
(rather than what you don't), it can be transformative to the
point of being life-changing. It spells the end of Sunday-night
doom, Monday-morning blues and Hump-day. It's time for
the scales to fall from our eyes and for us to remember that
our jobs should work for us, not the other way round.

ACKNOWLEDGEMENTS

An extra special thank you to two people – my husband Bear who provided the catering for this whole endeavour, and put up with endless tantrums, freak-outs and melt-downs along the way, and my mum Jackie, who's first job after retirement was part-time research assistant, part-time sub editor, part-time transcription service, and full-time cheerleader for BETA.

I also need to thank my amazing agent Bryony who hand-held me through the entire process and shaped my book proposal into something great, Charlotte and the team at Coronet who have been absolutely fantastic. And, of course, the dozens of women who gave up their precious time to tell me about their experiences in the workplace.

Finally, all the great women I've worked with who've been Alpha, Beta and everything in between. I literally couldn't have done it without you.